THE ABINGDON WOMEN'S PREACHING ANNUAL

Series 1

Year C

THE ABINGDON WOMEN'S PREACHING ANNUAL

Series 1

Year C

COMPILED AND EDITED BY

Jana L. Childers and Lucy A. Rose

Abingdon Press
Nashville

THE ABINGDON WOMEN'S PREACHING ANNUAL

ISBN 0-687-058481
ISSN 1086-8240

97 98 99 00 01 02 03 04 05 06—10 9 8 7 6 5 4 3 2 1

MANUFACTURED IN THE UNITED STATES OF AMERICA

To

Gary Dreibelbis

and

Gerry Cook

Contents

Introduction

I call it a miracle, a small one to be sure and one steeped in ambiguity—what miracle isn't? But even as I spoke on the telephone, I knew God was mysteriously at work. For others the phone call would be a coincidence, the result of chance, good fortune, luck, or Carl Jung's synchronicity. It was, after all, just a phone call.

My assignment was to write this introduction. Everything was at hand—a manuscript to peruse, paper for writing, two well-sharpened pencils (sometimes for me the computer inhibits inspiration). I had written a tentative opening sentence when the phone rang. A clergywoman and former student was calling to chat briefly about a journal article on preaching I had written. She wanted to report on a meeting she had attended with several other preachers and a few seminary professors, eight besides herself—all men. The subject of my article arose during the meeting and the consensus of the eight was that they didn't get it. "But," she exclaimed, "I did! My congregation is always saying to me 'You preach so differently.' " Then she mused, "All those sermons you get canned, unless they're written by women I can't use them."

She didn't know I was in the process of writing an introduction to a collection of sermon briefs, reflections, and liturgical resources by women who preach. She didn't know I was revisiting the question, Do women preach differently? I could almost hear God chuckling in the wings. And I felt a tug at my heart: If only all of life, if only all of life for everyone in the whole world, could be so congruent, so on time, so infused with God's shalom. I call it a miracle.

So what's different about this collection? Perhaps in part it is the world these pages invite us to enter, a world that so values faith and doubt, heart and head, texts and personal experiences (Cartesian oppositions that really belong together) that I, for one, felt wholly valued so that I was free to risk being touched by the sanctifying breath of God's spirit.

Let me describe some of the characters who inhabit this world, created by these sermon briefs, reflections, and liturgical resources. Here are friends and strangers: Mary Magdalene waiting for the morning so she can anoint the dead body of Jesus; Archbishop Oscar Romero; lepers, nobodies, and all those on the margins of society; those with "broken, withered, wild bodies and broken, poisoned, lost spirits" (McDougle); immigrants who remember "the hardships they suffered, the language they spoke, the music they played, and the food they ate" (Wenig); those afraid of death . . . and of life; all those—all of us—who hunger to hear the Good News.

We, the readers, are invited to become characters by bringing our faith in the Resurrection and our resistance to resurrection life or bringing our memories evoked by the death of Sapphire, the two-month-old hamster. Here in this world, our status as believers and decision makers is respected; we are not told what to do or think or believe. Rather, in the words of the clergywoman on the other end of the phone line, we are given "the opportunity to figure it out for [our]selves."

God also is a character in the world of these pages. In Jesus, God "takes on the uniform of humanity and is born naked in the world on a stable floor" (McDougle). In Jesus, God comes like a health inspector visiting a restaurant or like "an unscheduled train pulling into a station" so that "those who are ready and see it can get on" and "those who do not cannot catch it once it leaves" (González). God in these pages is a character who makes a difference "both in our lives and in our deaths" (Hogan).

Emerging from the world of these pages, I remember that miracles do happen because God is a character both in the written texts we read and in life—worlds we help to construct with names like "miracle" or "luck."

Lucy A. Rose
Lent 1996
Decatur, Georgia

First Sunday of Advent

Mary Ellen Azada

Jeremiah 33:14-16: Jeremiah proclaims a message of judgment to those in exile. In the midst of this proclamation, while he himself is being confined in the court, Jeremiah delivers words of hope. The phrase "The days are surely coming" is repeated five times in chapters 30–33, pointing to the days when Israel will no longer be in exile.

Psalm 25:1-10: This is one of several acrostic poems found in the book of Psalms. The message in Psalm 25 is similar to the message in Jeremiah; God's mercy and love are steadfast, even when we have transgressed.

I Thessalonians 3:9-13: This letter to the Thessalonian church is a letter of encouragement and thanksgiving for their faithfulness. Paul commends them as examples and expresses his joy for their steadfastness in the midst of his own suffering.

Luke 21:25-36: This passage focuses on Jesus' prophetic word about the destruction of Jerusalem, and the tumultuous times that will occur prior to it. Although we read images of doom, of heavens being shaken, and of waves roaring, the Son of Man prevails.

REFLECTIONS

I wonder how it is that I have been in the church since the age of five and did not "experience" Advent until after my college years. Of course we celebrated Christmas, but Advent either got swept to the side in the excitement of Christmas or it just didn't leave an impression on me. I truly don't know which is the case—loss of memory or no real teaching on it!

Advent, the time of preparation and waiting for the birth of the Christ Child, somehow has lost its meaning in the postmodern world in which we live. As I reflect upon these passages that move us to focus not only on the birth of Jesus, but also on the Second Coming of Jesus, I am struck by the circumstances in our lives that mitigate our sense of expectance.

In a society of comfort and affluence, the need for a Savior outside ourselves is hindered by the things that clutter our lives. We have become accustomed to a set of values that urge us to "do it on our own." When Jesus was born, it was different. There was a profound and deep anticipation of the Messiah among the Jews. John the Baptist's arrival stirred this longing for a Messiah, as people wondered if this man was the prophet whose voice "[cried] out in the wilderness" (Isa. 40:3).

Perhaps in this age of high tech communication, given our ability to view the suffering of the world at such a rapid speed, we have become desensitized to much of our own pain and the pain of the world. Our sense of expectance has shrunk because we are out of touch with our need for healing. For us perhaps the Advent season is not only a season for anticipating the birth of our Lord and the return of our Savior, but a season to acknowledge our need for God.

A SERMON BRIEF

In a day of religious freedom, a young man is rejected because of his faith. Because he has turned his heart to God, he is now without a family. In a day of progressive thinking and at a time when we are taught to strive to be whatever we desire, a friend tells me her decision to be in Christian ministry is unacceptable to her family. In a day of acceptance, I sit with colleagues in ministry of different denominations, only to feel silenced and judged for following a call that they believe has not been offered me.

The cost of discipleship is high. What we experience today as Christians in this country may not be the same kind of persecution our forefathers and mothers in Thessalonica knew, but it is painful.

The apostle Paul, having been directed very clearly by the Holy Spirit not to go to Asia or Bithynia, receives a vision of a man beckoning him to cross over to Macedonia. Paul, in obedience, takes a ship and sails from one continent to another, landing in Philippi. There he meets Lydia, who eagerly accepts the Good News of Jesus Christ and responds by being baptized.

Abruptly, after such a positive initial reception, Paul finds himself facing opposition in Philippi, so he moves on to Thessalonica. In Thessalonica, after hearing Paul preach and teach in the synagogue, some were persuaded and became followers of Christ. (There were, of course, also others who reacted out of jealousy and persecuted Paul and his companions.) To those who heard the Good News and responded with the commitment of their lives, Paul writes this letter.

There is something about reading the accounts of Paul's missionary journey to Thessalonica (see also Acts 17) that is heartwarming. One gets the sense that real relationships were formed. There is an authenticity about these scriptures. The relationships pictured here ring true, reminding us of individuals we might have met on a short-term mission project and of our attempts to keep in touch with them by letter.

In his letter to the Thessalonians, Paul encourages them, saying that he continually receives reports of their faithfulness and their examples of living out their faith. In the midst of persecution, they not only have maintained their faith but have continued to grow in love. Instead of shrinking in fear and isolating themselves from the world, their love has increased. No wonder Paul writes, "How can we thank God enough for you in return for all the joy that we feel . . . because of you?" (3:9). What an encouragement their lives must have been to Paul!

Later in the letter we read that among these faithful folks—for whom Paul is so grateful—there are some who are concerned about the delay of Jesus' return (I Thess. 4:13-18). To them Paul writes like an understanding parent, eager to tell the Thessalonians to persevere despite their struggles. Just as they have persevered through their persecutions, they may persevere through their waiting.

It is appropriate advice for us as well. We who also wait for the return of our Lord should not be idle. Rather we should wait continuing the work that God has given to us, to grow deeper in our love for others. There are many examples of people of faith "persevering." We have only to look around us.

As a child growing up, I moved frequently. As I continued to attend Sunday school and worship services faithfully, each church helped open my eyes a bit more to the potential of the Body of Christ. In missionary churches abroad, military chaplaincies, denominational and nondenominational congregations, big churches, and house churches, I have seen tremendous acts of love and faithfulness.

In the church where I currently work, there are models of Christian love that I have never seen elsewhere. Of course, there continue to be areas where we can grow, but I have learned much about the love of Christ from the example of these brothers and sisters in Christ. For example, when a fellow believer is suffering from illness, a member takes that person into her home until the person recovers. A married couples' group provides meals on a rotating basis to help an ailing member for an extended period of time. For one who is housebound, a member visits regularly. A teenage deacon visits one who is ill—even making a visit on the member's last day of life. A woman who is struggling herself, continually seeks out others in need of friendship. These faithful members give of their time, talents, and tithes quietly. Without recognition, they lovingly live out the example of Christ. I stand in awe.

We have much to do as we wait for our Lord. We are called not to wait on a hill, not to sit idly by until the day of Christ comes, but to grow lives deep and rich in love. So during this Advent season when our thoughts are filled with "What to give her or him?" we might also do a mental check of the depth of our love for him or for her. With Advent we are beckoned to move forward into the future, growing more in love. In the same way that the church at Thessalonica discovered that they could persevere through persecution and the wait for Christ's return, so we must learn to let nothing prevent us from continuing in God's love. In this season, we are called to consider what it means to be a follower of Christ and what it means to live lives grown deep in love.

Suggestions for Worship

Call to Worship (based on Psalm 25)

LEADER: To you, O Lord, we lift our souls.

PEOPLE: O God, in you we put our trust.

LEADER: Make us to know your ways,

PEOPLE: Open our hearts and teach us.

LEADER: You are the God of our salvation,

PEOPLE: For you we wait all day long.

LEADER: Good and upright is the Lord.

**PEOPLE: We are mindful of your mercy, O Lord,
and of your steadfast love.**

LEADER: O God, in you we put our trust.

Prayer of Confession

Holy One of God,
Forgive us for we are quick to stray.
We seek that which does not bring us fulfillment.
We acknowledge that in this season of giving,
We are tempted by that which is made by human hands.
Help us, O God, to remain faithful to you.
Keep us ever focused on all that is eternal—
    on love, mercy, and faithfulness.
Direct our sights to Jesus, to his birth, and to his return.
To the glory of God Almighty. Amen.

Assurance of Pardon (based on Jer. 33:15; I Thess. 3:13)

The Lord is just and righteous. The Lord will save us from our sins. Believe the Good News! In Jesus Christ our sins are forgiven! And God will strengthen our hearts in holiness. Amen.

Benediction (based on Luke 21:36; I Thess. 3:12-13)

Be alert at all times. Love one another. And may the Lord make you increase and abound in love for all and so strengthen your hearts in holiness that you may be blameless before God at the coming of our Lord Jesus with all the saints. Go in peace.

Second Sunday of Advent

Carter Shelley

Malachi 3:1-4: The messenger of the covenant is promised, one like a refiner's fire and fullers' soap.

Luke 1:68-79: The Benedictus of Zechariah, John the Baptist's father.

Philippians 1:3-11: Paul's prayer for his Philippian partners in the gospel.

Luke 3:1-6: Luke's introduction of John the Baptist.

REFLECTIONS

An overall theme of the four lectionary passages is the call to humanity to be righteous. An affirmation that God is present and at work in present events also links these texts.

A key word for Malachi (and one that we encounter in the words of almost every prophet who precedes John the Baptist) is "righteousness." An interesting addition that Malachi's words make to the second Sunday of Advent is the notion of presenting something to God. Those whose lives are purified by the Lord's messenger will not present gold and silver to God but themselves. They will present themselves as spiritually and ethically pure servants who understand that what will please God is not hard metals but lives of mettle and merit.

The theme of knowledge, which is important in Luke 1:77, also appears in Philippians: "This is my prayer, that your love may overflow more and more with knowledge and full insight" (1:9). Insight into what? Paul doesn't say what. Paul says what for: "to help you determine what is best, so that in the day of Christ you may be pure and blameless." Here Paul provides a link to Malachi's purifying metals image and to John's call to repentance.

"To determine what is best" is a hopeful word. It suggests the possibility of living such a life, of discovering such a truth, thanks to Christ and to love. When love is tempered by knowledge and full insight into God's will, it will help the Philippians determine what is best. This kind of righteousness that Paul urges will no longer be demanded by prophets and priests who can't help despairing of it ever happening. Now, thanks to the "harvest of righteousness that comes through Jesus Christ," believers can attain it.

A SERMON BRIEF

Although we did not read the earlier portion of Luke 1, you'll remember it tells of the angel messenger's appearance to Zechariah while he is in the Temple's holy of holies. Most of us know that part of the story. We know that Zechariah and his wife, Elizabeth, are blameless and righteous people. We know they have no children because Elizabeth is barren and they are both getting on in years. We know that while they have not given up on God, they have given up on the possibility of parenting children of their own. We also know that being barren in biblical times was about as painful and tragic a bereavement as any couple could experience. We know this because it is a biblical theme that is played over and over again.

The childless Abraham uproots his whole household to follow his God into wilderness wandering. Abraham is promised not only a great land but great descendants through good old Sarah who's been a real trooper in travel but a wipeout in the child-production department.

We know Jacob's wife Rebekah was jealous of her sister Leah's fertility because a patriarch's wife is only as good as the sons she produces.

We remember Hannah weeping to God at Shiloh, praying to God to please give her a child and promising to give the boy back to God when he is old enough to be dedicated to the Lord's service.

We know these stories. We know these women. We feel their sense of emptiness because the Bible insists that we recognize how much their lives and their meaning were tied to the birthing and raising of children. We also know that each of these women is finally blessed by God with a son. And not just any son, but illustrious sons whose names will be celebrated in Judaism, Christianity, and Islam: Isaac, the patriarch; Joseph, adviser to pharaohs; Samuel, judge of Israel and prophet to two kings.

To be a barren woman in Old Testament days was to be a miserable woman, an unfulfilled woman, an inadequate woman, a failure. To be barren is to be empty, to have no hope for the future, to be a failure, to have no hope of life after one's own death. And if, as all devout Jews believed, life is God's greatest gift, then to be barren means one has been given only half a life because one can't reproduce it.

All of these theological and emotional messages were there for Jewish couples who had no children. So, when we read Luke 1:6-7, we understand that behind the dispassionate, straightforward words of the author, there reside years of heartache for Zechariah and Elizabeth: "Both of them were righteous before God, living blamelessly according to all the commandments and regulations of the Lord. But they had no children, because Elizabeth was barren, and both were getting on in years."

Benedictus. It's the Latin word which means "blessed."

Benedictus. It's the first word the no-longer-mute Zechariah speaks. "Blessed be the Lord God of Israel."

Benedictus. John, their son, is a blessing to Elizabeth and Zechariah because he brings love, joy, and life into their previously barren home.

Benedictus. John, their son, is a blessing upon them from God because his birth is an acknowledgment that their righteous lives and dedication to God and God's commandments have been observed and rewarded.

Benedictus. John, their son, is a blessing to the Jewish people, who once again need a word of judgment and hope from one who comes as prophet, herald, and witness to God's promised Savior.

Benedictus. John, their son, is a blessing because he will assist in broadening the scope of God's blessing to all peoples and nations: "All flesh shall see the salvation of God."

Benedictus. John, their son, is himself blessed to be placed so near in God's plan to one Luke describes as the Christ, the Son of God.

To be barren is to be empty, to have no hope for the future, to be a failure, to have no hope of life after one's own death. And if, as all devout Jews believed, life is God's greatest gift, then to be barren means one has been given only half a life because one can't reproduce it.

To be blessed is to experience joy, love, and life. It is to have one's life acknowledged and rewarded. It is to recognize God's prophet and heed his or her word. It is to know that salvation is possible here and now.

What makes the difference between barrenness and blessing? God's intervention. God's action. God's graciousness. The infant John and the adult John are both a blessing from God, a gift to John's parents and a gift to God's people.

We are barren. Some of us live the tragedy of barrenness in the biblical sense. For reasons of infertility, chronic illness, or repeated miscarriages, our wombs remain empty and our hearts very sad.

We are barren. A thirty-five-year-old father only sees his children two weekends per month, because the court has decreed that they live with their mother and new stepfather. We are barren when we cannot be with children we have helped to create.

We are barren. When we still love our marriage partners but no longer share the same goals or values and do not know how to reach each other anymore.

We are barren. When we live by ourselves and assume that such a life offers only isolation and loneliness.

We are barren. When we live as single parents worn down by hard work, children's demands, and the weighty reality of more bills than money with which to pay them.

We are barren. When our emotional energies are depleted with feelings of hate and resentment and revenge against former spouses or current foes.

We are barren. When we seek life's purpose in the wrong places: money, a job, sex, children, or fame.

We are barren. When we forget God and focus upon ourselves, seeking life's meaning within ourselves.

We know about our barrenness. Where is our blessing? To be blessed is to experience joy, love, and life. It is to have one's life acknowledged and rewarded. It is to recognize God's prophet and heed his or her word. It is to know that salvation is possible here and now.

The final words of Zechariah's blessing are words of hope, words of peace:

> "By the tender mercy of our God,
>   the dawn from on high will break upon us,
> to give light to those who sit in darkness
>   and in the shadow of death,
>   to guide our feet into the way of peace." (Luke 1:78-79)

"The *Benedictus* links the promise of salvation and redemption insepara-bly to the achievement of peace" (R. Alan Culpepper, *Luke and John,* vol. 9 of *The New Interpreter's Bible* [Nashville: Abingdon Press, 1995], 60). As we prepare once more for Jesus' birth on Christmas day, let us examine anew the barren places in our lives. Examine them. Grieve over them. And give them to God to expose and redeem, that you and I may find peace in our souls and joy in our hearts.

Benedictus. Blessed is the Lord God of Israel!

SUGGESTIONS FOR WORSHIP

Call to Worship (Luke 3:4c-6)

LEADER: Prepare the way of the Lord, make his paths straight.

PEOPLE: **Every valley shall be filled, and every mountain and hill shall be made low,**

LEADER: And the crooked shall be made straight, and the rough ways made smooth;

PEOPLE: **And all flesh shall see the salvation of God.**

Prayer of Confession

Parent of all children and Lord of us all,
We want this Advent to be joyful and free of guilt and obligations,
and you forgive us.
We want more money, more security, more certainty in our lives,
and you forgive us.
We buy guns to keep us safe on our streets and in our homes,
and you forgive us.
We want to close our borders, limit immigration, and keep America
for the Americans,
and you forgive us.
We want a world that is at peace but refuse to accept its social or economic price,
and you forgive us.
We want Jesus to remain forever a baby in a manger, gentle as a child,
and you forgive us.
We want tender mercies, not honest prophets,
and you forgive us.
Convict us with the Baptist's words and claim us again in Christ
Jesus' name as you forgive us today. Amen.

Benediction (Luke 1:78-79)

By the tender mercy of our God,
    the dawn from on high will break upon us,
to give light to those who sit in darkness
    and in the shadow of death,
      to guide our feet into the way of peace.

Third Sunday of Advent

Carter Shelley

Zephaniah 3:14-20: Israel is invited to sing and rejoice for the Lord will save, gather, and restore the people.

Isaiah 12:2-6: The prophet celebrates God as "my salvation," "my strength and my might," and anticipates a day of joy and thanksgiving for all Israel.

Philippians 4:4-7: Paul reminds the church to rejoice, to let their gentleness be known, not to worry, and to let their requests be known to God. And they are promised the peace of God.

Luke 3:7-18: John the Baptist addresses the crowds who gather around him, and the crowds question him, "What shall we do?"

REFLECTIONS

I particularly like Luke's version of John the Baptist's ministry because it is so pointed and specific. It is also incredibly incendiary. It reminds me of revivalist ministers who verbally abuse their congregations. It reminds me of the people who seem to lap such abuse up and are thankful for those who tell them what awful people they are. It fits in with my belief that most people don't understand grace. They don't know what it means to be truly loved, accepted by God, and given infinite second chances. This message is especially acute and vital to women. We tend to undervalue ourselves:

"I'm just a housewife."

"I'm Mrs. John P. Smith. My own name is unimportant."

"I'm not smart; I just work hard."

"If I had been smarter, sexier, prettier, he might not have left."

We judge ourselves so harshly; we hardly need help from God or male prophets to tell us we are bad. Self-loathing is a natural state of being for many women in many cultures, including the one into which John the Baptist and Jesus were born. Women were not counted among one's blessings. One of the important ways that the Old and New Testaments transcend their time is in naming and telling the stories of women.

John's message is one of judgment and confrontation. Yet it is described in v. 18 as "good news," which, of course, it is to those who believe the teachings and ministries of the Messiah when he comes. Christianity in its pure form can be good news for women especially. It provides a way for human beings to relate that is governed not by power and weapons but by love and sharing.

A Sermon Brief

Harry walked into the dining room. He held a bouquet of two dozen roses. "These are for you, honey," he said, handing the roses to his wife. "I'm really sorry about last night. I've felt awful about it all day. I could hardly concentrate in the directors' meeting. I was too upset to eat lunch. Do you forgive me?"

Janey took the roses with a tremulous smile. She was afraid to tell him she'd spent the morning at the hospital, that this time she had two cracked ribs. She knew Harry was sorry. Harry always apologized afterward.

"You brood of vipers! Who warned you to flee from the wrath to come? Bear fruits worthy of repentance. Do not begin to say to yourselves, 'I am a churchgoer and a fine, upstanding citizen.' Even now the ax is lying at the root of the trees; every tree therefore that does not bear good fruit is cut down and thrown into the fire."

Alice came to the breakfast table bleary-eyed and exhausted. Her dormmates looked at her in surprise. Usually Alice was a sound sleeper.

"What's up? You make a B on your German paper?" Nancy asked. Alice was an ace at German.

"No. I just couldn't get the sight of that woman and her children out of my mind. I was up all night worrying about them."

"What children?" asked Helen.

"You weren't there," answered Nancy. "The Christmas party the church sponsored for disadvantaged families yesterday evening."

"I just couldn't quit seeing them. That little girl couldn't have been more than four, and her two brothers were even younger. They didn't have coats or gloves or hats. Their little fingers were so red from the cold. Their mother looked younger than us. She said she'd had to sell the children's coats because she ran out of food. Her English was so bad I had to ask her to repeat herself three times. All we had for them was a bunch of stupid little games and candy. We didn't have any nutritious food, just cupcakes and cookies and punch. I thought people like that got welfare. I thought there were food stamps and stuff."

"There is. My mom volunteers once a week at Hope House at home," said Nancy. "She says welfare families never have enough to live on. They're always coming in for help paying bills. They come in all the time for food and clothes."

"Seems like it'd be easier to work than to live on welfare," Helen inserted.

"Yeah. Well, it's not that simple. If women work, they have to pay for child care, and they don't usually get paid enough to pay for child care and pay their bills. It's not like they've got college degrees or anything," Nancy said.

"Well, I don't want to think about it anymore. It makes me feel awful. Those kids have no future, no future at all. The daughter will get pregnant just like her mother, and her brothers will grow up and become drug addicts or crooks. It makes me so sick and hopeless."

"Good morning, ladies," chirped a fourth student joining their breakfast table. "Alice, you must have been really sleepy to have walked off without this." The girl handed Alice a wrapped Christmas present.

"What is it?" Alice asked.

"It's your first present from your Secret Santa. It was lying outside your door where anyone could have taken it."

"Oh, thanks. Gee, I've got to find time to drive downtown today and get some stuff. I forgot today was the first day for Secret Santas. Thanks for reminding me, Melissa."

"Well! Obviously you're not my Secret Santa," Melissa said. "I got a really fabulous Hootie and the Blowfish CD from mine."

"No fair! All I got was a can of cashews," Nancy protested. "Of course, I love cashews. They'll come in handy during cramming for exams."

"*Whoever has two coats must share with anyone who has none; and whoever has food must do likewise.*"

Jack toyed with the take-out Chinese food on his plate. Steven had a basketball game tonight. His first game ever. He'd sounded so excited and eager on the phone and then so close to tears when Jack had told him he couldn't make it. Nine years old. Surely he was too old to cry by now. For crying out loud! What was Jack supposed to do? He'd never make partner if he didn't put in the hours—twelve hours a day. That's what it took if he wanted to win cases and add to the firm's grosses.

It'd be a whole lot easier if Marge weren't equally stretched. Between her medical practice and his equally demanding law practice, they made plenty of money. What they didn't have was time. Tonight she'd drive Steven to his game but wouldn't be able to stay because she had to take the twins to their pageant rehearsal and then go back to the hospital to check on a patient who had had a stroke earlier in the day. Neither of them would see Steven play. In fact neither of them had been there when Elizabeth took her first step or Cindy spoke her first word. Jack couldn't remember the last time he'd spent an entire day with his family.

When he was home he usually ended up yelling at the kids to "Get out of here! I'm working," or else he was too tired to do anything but sleep. Cindy's first grade picture of her family had included the dog, her twin sister, her brother, and Karen, the baby-sitter. When Jack had asked her where he and her mother were, Cindy had said, "You're asleep on the couch. I don't know how to draw couches yet. Mummy's with someone sick."

"What then should we do?"

Guilt isn't good enough. But sometimes we confuse bad feelings and sleepless nights with repentance. We think that if we watch the evening news and are brought to tears by the sight of homeless children in our city or maimed bodies in some foreign land that we are caring, compassionate people. We fool ourselves into believing that fretting about poverty or worrying about our children is the same thing as doing something. John the Baptist knew better. He knew that repentance isn't repentance unless there is a change in human behavior.

"What then should we do?"

Quit beating your wife.

"What then should we do?"

"Whoever has two coats must share with anyone who has none."

"What then should we do?"

Spend more time with your children.

Repentance means turning around, going in another direction, not repeating past sins and past behaviors, changing. Guilt is not repentance. Guilt is a feeling, not an action. It's a feeling that we sometimes confuse with repentance because when we feel bad, when we feel guilty, we also feel as though we have done something.

The Old Testament prophets—Amos, Hosea, Isaiah, Zephaniah, Jeremiah—knew the difference between feelings and action. Like their New Testament brother John the Baptist, they understood that repentance requires a recognition of sin, a determination to live differently, and a genuine change of direction in one's life—actually turning and going in a new direction.

Repentance involves Harry's admitting he's out of control, getting counseling, and joining a support group for abusive spouses. Repentance involves Alice's figuring out a way that she can do more than serve punch and cookies at a Christmas party for disadvantaged children. Repentance involves Jack and Marge figuring out how to cut their workloads so they can spend time with their children.

Prophets, priests, ministers, and Saviors don't enter our world to make us feel guilty. They are sent by God to call us to our senses, to point us in the right direction, and to give us the courage to go where they are leading. They do not ask more of us than they ask of themselves. Prophets, priests, ministers, and Saviors point the way, know the route, and proclaim the trip is worth the effort.

For the good news is repentance is possible. Isaiah declares the Good News: "God is my salvation; I will trust, and will not be afraid, for the LORD GOD is my strength and my might; he has become my salvation" (12:2). Zephaniah knows the Good News: "The LORD, your God, is in your midst, a warrior who gives victory; he will rejoice over you with gladness, he will renew you in his love" (3:17). John the Baptist proclaims Good News: "One who is more powerful than I is coming. . . . He will baptize you with the Holy Spirit and fire. His winnowing fork is in his hand . . . to gather the wheat into his granary" (3:16-17). Paul rejoices and records the Good News: "The Lord is near. . . . And the peace of God, which surpasses all understanding, will guard your hearts and your minds in Christ Jesus" (Phil. 4:5, 7).

Guilt is not good enough. Repentance, a change of heart, and a change in behavior are. Thanks be to God who loves us, the prophets who confront us, and the Messiah who saves us now and forevermore. Amen!

SUGGESTIONS FOR WORSHIP

Call to Worship (Isa. 12:4*b*-6 adapted)

LEADER: Give thanks to the LORD, call on his name;

PEOPLE: **Make known his deeds among the nations;**

LEADER: Proclaim that his name is exalted.

PEOPLE: **Sing praises to the LORD, for God has done gloriously;**

LEADER: Let this be known in all the earth.

PEOPLE: **Shout aloud and sing for joy, O inhabitant of Zion;**

LEADER: For great in your midst is the Holy One of Israel.

Prayer of Confession

Holy One of Israel, our Lord and our God, as citizens we want lower taxes but more benefits for ourselves and those whose miseries convict us. Forgive us, Lord, for wanting to have our cash and spend it, too.

As Christians we want to feel righteous and virtuous but we don't want to change our piety or our habits to make it so. Forgive us, Lord, for wanting to have our faith and neglect it, too.

As women and men, we want to be known as good parents, successful professionals, and cherished friends, but we are overwhelmed, overextended, and much on edge. Forgive us, Lord, for wanting to have it all and be human, too. Amen.

Assurance of Pardon (Zeph. 3:14-15; Isa. 12:2 adapted)

LEADER: Sing aloud, O daughter Zion; shout, O Israel!

Rejoice and exult with all your heart, O daughter Jerusalem!

The LORD has taken away the judgments against you;

God has turned away your enemies.

PEOPLE: **Surely God is my salvation;**

I will trust, and will not be afraid,

For the LORD GOD is my strength and my might;

God has become my salvation.

Benediction (Phil. 4:4-7)

Rejoice in the Lord always; again I will say, Rejoice. Let your gentleness be known to everyone. The Lord is near. Do not worry about anything, but in everything by prayer and supplication with thanksgiving let your requests be made known to God. And the peace of God, which surpasses all understanding, will guard your hearts and your minds in Christ Jesus.

Fourth Sunday of Advent

Gail McDougle

Micah 5:2-5*a*: Micah speaks of a day when little Bethlehem, least among the clans of Judah, will be the birthplace of one who will rule over Israel. The one born will not only feed his flock in power and majesty, but will, himself, "be peace."

Psalm 80:1-7: This psalm voices the community's distress at a time when God's smoldering anger with them makes God seem absent. Having been fed on the "bread of tears," the people implore God to shepherd, restore, and smile upon them.

Hebrews 10:5-10: The writer of Hebrews asserts the inefficacy of the sacrifices of "bull's blood and goat's blood" to take away sin, and contrasts it with the efficacy of Jesus' self-offering.

Luke 1:39-55: Following the angel's surprise announcement, Mary quickly heads for the hill country and Elizabeth's house. The two kinswomen rejoice in their otherwise mysterious, even troubling, pregnancies. Elizabeth seems certain Mary's motherhood is most blessed. And Mary exults: she sings of a God who befriends those in low places and who turns the tables on the rich and powerful.

REFLECTIONS

Something strange is afoot in the first chapter of Luke's Gospel: a visiting angel, a "spiritual" conception, a pregnant virgin, a pregnant post-menopausal woman, a leaping fetus, and talk of being the Lord's mother.

Mary and Elizabeth rejoice in that strangeness and experience it as happening right there in their gynecological systems.

Mary's response is to sing, but it is not the standard lullaby. Mary's song is about a God who blesses lowly nobodies and ne'er-do-wells and turns the tables on blue bloods and power brokers. Kings wait tables, while servants feast. Mary sings that God is about to work a surprising mercy, delivering on a promise made centuries before to Abraham and Sarah. The lyric itself is a patchwork quilt of Jewish scripture, with many phrases from the psalms and remarkably similar to Hannah's song (I Sam. 2:1-10).

Of course, the wonder of this text for the preacher is that it exists at all. Mark and John do not address this part of Jesus' story. Matthew does, but he takes a different tack. History? Did it happen just this way? Who were Luke's sources sixty-odd years later? With what forces and issues was the emerging Christian movement struggling when Luke wrote? At least one thing is clear: though Jesus and John are linked from birth and are kin, Jesus' birth is the more remarkable in every way. Foremost, it is the product of a divine-human conception. The text reads like a Lukan attempt to distinguish Jesus' identity and ministry from John's.

But that misses the bigger picture of Luke's story: that the surprising mercy God worked did not descend from a cloud on high or on clay tablets, but entered the world through the dark, narrow channel of a peasant girl's birth canal. God's mercy would wear human flesh—lowly Galilean human flesh, at that. For Luke, God's activity in Jesus had a this-worldly, here-and-now nature that flew in the face of that world's power structure. A peasant Jewish girl was caught up in God's great drama. No wonder she sang!

A SERMON BRIEF

Mary's troubled heart undoubtedly sent her speeding to older and wise Elizabeth. She was trying to quiet the storm of emotion rumbling through her mind and body. Is this good news or bad? Am I to rejoice or die of shame? What will I tell my family and friends? How will this all turn out?

The mind's eye can see the embrace, the exchange, the bewilderment, the wonderment, the connecting, the bonding: Mary and Elizabeth straining to comprehend, to fathom the new reality alive and growing in their bodies. It is the sisterhood of two women, joined in fear and anticipation, who find themselves caught up in a drama of immense proportions that has made a very personal and visceral claim on their bodies.

Luke says Mary broke into song. She joins that long tradition of Jewish women—the Hannahs and the Miriams—who sing in response to the mysterious workings of the Holy One in the middle of human history. Here at the beginning of Jesus' life story, Mary's lyric provides a poignant interpretation of the life that would come into the world from her womb.

The singer asserts that God is about to work a powerful reversal in human affairs. And she, herself, is the first proof of that assertion. Mary is the "lowly handmaid" who is agent to God's work. God is not working through the power elite of her world, but through her. Galilean, peasant, woman: none of these locate Mary in any category of power or prestige whatsoever. "Lowly" gets it right: Galilean, not Judean; peasant, not aristocrat; woman, not man. The singer is the first clue that a reversal is underway.

Mary's song tells us that God's power—not the proud human power system in charge in Mary's day—would be revealed. And that revelation would find princes dethroned, and the wealthy without, while the lowly would know exaltation and the hungry satisfaction. Whatever reversals God might be working would transform this real world of rulers and rich people, disadvantaged and hungry people.

Which, of course, is precisely Luke's understanding of the life that would be born into the world through Mary's labor. This song is Luke's prelude to the life of Jesus. And what does the prelude tell us? That God in Jesus is radically invested in this real world and in the real-life struggles of flesh-and-blood people: so invested, in fact, that divinity takes on the uniform of humanity and is born naked in the world on a stable floor. It may be unsophisticated and messy, but Luke says it is how God decided to begin that great reversal.

How can we read Luke—how can we hear Mary's song—and not know that God's investment is with this blue-green-brown earth and its people? God's life-giving commitment is not to some phantom planet or some ghostly distillation of us or some afterlife. God is with us here—active here—invested here, involved here, committed here to this life on this earth—and not with just the rich and powerful, but with the peasant, the poor, and the destitute. This earth is the birthplace and the workplace of Jesus, the location of God's ultimate concern.

So what?

So—this life and this earth and the human struggles and the human condition are the objects of God's concern and God's love. Mary's song proclaims the divine assessment: human life is precious and worthy. God invests in it!

So—the power structures of Mary's world and ours are not necessarily those in concert with the activity of God. Mary's song serves notice to the arrogant that ruling power and wealth are not necessarily God-ordained and God-serving. If the past is any predictor of the present and future, God may be working in unexpected places with unexpected people to bring about unexpected results that will transform the world. God surprises us!

So—the ministry of the one born to Mary begins in marginal circumstances. We should not be surprised to discover that it continues to take place among the marginalized people. Jesus of Nazareth, a peasant himself, walks among the marginalized, heals the marginalized, calls the marginalized. He invites them to a table where their societal isolation dies and their life begins.

So—there is a countercultural quality to this song, this story. God's activity is not confined to the establishment, no matter how "religious" it believes itself to be. The mysterious love of God for the world is not confined by human perceptions of what makes good sense, what is appropriate, what is the best way to make things happen. The mysterious love of God is simply that: mysterious. No wonder Mary sang!

SUGGESTIONS FOR WORSHIP

Call to Worship

Let us sing, as Mary sang,
    about the mysterious work of God
    in the here and now.
Let us praise, as Mary praised,
    the mercy of God
    to those who are nobodies.
Let us rejoice, as Mary rejoiced,
    that God is not limited
    by the way things are.
Let us worship, as Mary worshiped,
    the God whose love is able
    to do the impossible!

Prayer of Dedication

With hope in our hearts that we may be caught up, like Mary, in the great drama of your love, we bring these gifts to you, O God.

May those who live on the margins know the bounty of your grace and mercy through the stewardship of these gifts.

Remembering Jesus' self-giving, we pray. Amen.

Benediction

May your experience of God's love fill you with song and may your deep trust in God free you to sing it! Amen.

Holy Name of Jesus

Charlotte McGruder Abram

Numbers 6:22-27: God makes provisions to give the children the Lord's name. In the priestly tradition, Moses is instructed to direct Aaron and succeeding generations of priests to speak specific words of blessing through which the Lord's name will be put upon the people.

Psalm 8: This psalm praises the glorious name and majesty of God and celebrates the dignity God bestows upon humans.

Philippians 2:9-13: This reading begins with the last half of an ancient hymn of praise which confesses that "Jesus Christ is Lord." This name, "that is above every name" (v. 9) was bestowed by God.

Galatians 4:4-7: This text complements the Gospel lesson of the day. Through it we revisit the birth narrative. It confirms that through Jesus, God redeems us and adopts us as children.

Luke 2:15-21: As Luke's birth narrative concludes, we move with the shepherds from the fields as they visit the holy family. They share the message revealed to them concerning Mary's child. A pensive Mary treasures these words of confirmation in her heart. The text concludes with the holy family obediently observing the laws of Moses by circumcising and naming the baby the name the angels forespoke, "Jesus" (v. 21).

REFLECTIONS

My oldest brother recently embraced the Muslim faith. As a result of this life-altering event, he legally adopted a Muslim name to denote his new identity. Some in our family have been slow in adjusting to this change. Others have refused to even try. Yet, regardless of how others feel, we do have the right to name our reality.

Through naming our different realities, women, racial ethnics, and others plant seeds of transformation and chip away at racism, sexism, and classism. Growing up, I did not see women in the pastoral ministry. As time passed, more and more women named their reality, saying, "I am a preacher/pastor." They named themselves such, even though others tried to make them deny that reality. From Jarena Lee to Leontine Kelly, a host of women have pronounced a blessing on my life and enabled me to name my own reality as "called of God."

Naming is important. These texts offer a wonderful opportunity to learn about the power of naming as we exalt the name of Jesus. We can follow as God leads the way. God names a new reality for the Israelites, and runaway slaves become a people named after God. In and through the name of Jesus, God changes all of our realities. Because in Jesus' name we are now the freed and redeemed children of God. Like the ancient priest, we too are called to help people name this new reality for themselves.

A SERMON BRIEF

"Chub-tub," "Four-Eyes," "Crybaby," and, of course, "Tattletale" were a few of the names, the repeatable nicknames, my brothers called me. I won't share what I called them. As children, we risk getting in big trouble for calling each other derogatory names. Yet we persist in playing the name-calling game.

Perhaps you've called or been called a name before. Many groups of people, African-Americans, Hispanics, Chinese, Italian Americans, Polish Americans, and women, have been negatively nicknamed. Sections of cities are nicknamed "Shantytown" or "The Ghetto." Some congregations are nicknamed "Holy Rollers" and others "Blue Bloods," as we play the name-calling game.

Have you ever wondered why we take the names we are called so seriously? One might ask, "What's in a name?" There is plenty in a name. When we humans play the name-calling game, our attempts to control or define another person's behavior may lie behind the names we choose to call one another.

The names we are called affect our self-perception, our carriage of ourselves, and our actions. Maybe that's why we take name-calling so seriously.

During a public presentation, the speaker commented that he knew better than to address females as "ladies." His remarks reminded me of a time several years earlier when I was in seminary. In conversation, I referred to some other women as "ladies." Immediately another female student requested that I use the term "woman" rather than lady. I understood her request. In her experience, being called a "lady" was an attempt to make females, young and old, act in certain approved ways. It also encouraged females to forget about doing anything that was not ladylike.

At one time it was not considered "ladylike" to be too smart, especially smarter than the men in one's life. A lady would never dream of becoming a doctor, or a lawyer, a minister, an airline pilot, or—even today—a pro football player. A lady should only do and be what those who called her a lady thought she should do and be. I understood all of that. Yet I want my classmate and others to understand that there are other realities and experiences.

My African-American foremothers constantly lived with names that expressed societal disrespect. Sometimes they had to accept being called names that ranged from "gal" to the word that means a female canine. We were called those names as if they were our names. So when my husband or others call me a "lady," I receive it as a sign of respect. Yet as a sign of respect, I honor my sister's viewpoint for it is valid, and it is the reason I use the term "women" when speaking publicly. What's in a name? The attempt to control, define, demean, and confine can be expressed by and through the names we use.

Yet, when God gets in the name-calling game, as we witness in the text from Numbers, God calls us a name that builds up, blesses, and beckons us and others into a more positive future. God calls us a name that helps us perceive the true reality of our nature.

Here in the book of Numbers, can't you just see the children of Israel as they are gathered at the base of Mt. Sinai? Freedom was still new to them. All of their lives they had known themselves to be people who were treated as slaves. They answered to whatever name they were called, and they did whatever they were commanded to do. Their identity and self-image had been molded by their experience in Egypt. Yet, something would change in them and for them whenever the priest spoke the blessing, thus putting God's name on them. Backs were straightened, shoulders were pulled back, and bowed heads were lifted high, as they began to realize that they were no longer defined by the name "slave." They were becoming the people who carry the very name of the Lord. And if they carried the Lord's name, they knew they would carry the Lord's nature, for a person's name, they believed, revealed a person's nature. Their new name signified a change in their nature—like

Abram who became Abraham, Sarai who became Sarah, and Jacob who became Israel. God was instructing the priest to call this people to a new life of faith. What's in a name? A new identity and a new nature waiting to be called forth maybe in a name.

When God instructed Moses to tell Aaron and succeeding generations of priests to bless the people, thus putting the Lord's name on them, God was allowing the priest to call forth the best in the people. The priest named for them a part of their nature they themselves could not see. That can still happen today, through the priesthood of all believers.

I remember the time when I had not yet admitted to myself that I was called to pastoral ministry. I had been socialized to believe that women did not do that, especially in the African-American community. I tried to appease and bury the call by immersing myself in the joy I experienced as an active laywoman. All the while, several men and women in the congregation teasingly called me "Reverend." Even my pastor publicly named me as one called to pastoral ministry. They named in me what I could not yet see in myself. As I reflect back on that time, I realize that the pastor and congregation were calling forth and naming for me a new reality. We can all pass on the blessing by playing the name-calling game in ways that build up and affirm. What's in a name? New life, new hope, new joy, and the very nature of a person is in a name.

William Willimon says speaking a person's name evokes that person's presence. All we have to do, he says, is speak the name, and heart, mind, and memory do the rest. Speak the name of Moses, Harriet Tubman, Martin Luther King, Jr., or Jesus and all kinds of memories come to mind. He suggests that persons become present to us, in the here and now, "in the most explicit and intimate of ways" (William H. Willimon, *Advent/Christmas* [Minneapolis: Augsburg Fortress Press, 1993], p. 57).

Several years ago, a high school friend came to visit during one of her trips back home. This friend, who had renounced faith in Jesus during the "Black Power" movement of the '70s, shared a life-changing experience with me. She told me that on the drive home during a winter ice storm, her husband tapped the brakes to slow down a bit. The car slid out of control, turning around and careening backward toward the median. Suddenly, she heard herself call out the name "Jesus," a name she hadn't spoken in years, except in disdain. Immediately the car came back into control. What amazed her most about the whole incident was the fact that when she and her family were in mortal danger, she called the name "Jesus." That was something she thought she'd never do again. She spoke the name "Jesus" and heart, mind, and memory did the rest. She found her spirit in the presence of her Friend and Savior of yesteryear. She didn't know where all of that would lead. Yet she knew that there was something about her faith in Jesus that had not or would not let her go. What's in a name? There really is something in a name when that name is Jesus. Speak that name and fears subside. Speak that name and faith increases. Speak that name and faint hearts quicken.

What's in a name? There's salvation in the name of Jesus. Jesus, Mary's baby boy, is the Savior of the world. In the name of Jesus there is power to name and be named by God.

As we face this new year, even as we face each new day, and travel into each future moment, I encourage us to name and claim the name and nature by which God blesses us. I encourage us to do what Lydia Baxter suggested:

> Take the name of Jesus with you,
> child of sorrow and of woe;
> it will joy and comfort give you;
> take it then, where'er you go.
>
> Take the name of Jesus ever,
> as a shield from every snare;
> if temptations round you gather,
> breathe that holy name in prayer.
>
> Precious name, O how sweeet!
> Hope of earth and joy of heaven.

("Precious Name," *The United Methodist Hymnal* [Nashville: The United Methodist Publishing House, 1989], no. 536)

SUGGESTIONS FOR WORSHIP

Call to Worship (based on Psalm 8)

LEADER: Come! Let us praise the glorious name of God.

PEOPLE: **The glory of your name, O God, is known throughout the earth.**

LEADER: We look at the heavens, the moon and the stars,

PEOPLE: **We ask "Who are we, O God, that you should care for us?"**

LEADER: Yet you give us place of honor within your order of creation.

PEOPLE: **You entrust to our care the works of your hands.**

ALL: **O Lord, our God, how glorious is your name in all the earth.**

Prayer of Confession

Loving God, we know that in Jesus' name you gather all peoples and nations into one. Through faith in Jesus' name, you graciously offer salvation, adopting us as your own. Yet we confess that too often we name ourselves and others in ways that divide rather than unite. We swallow the gracious words of blessing which you place in our hearts to share. Forgive us, we pray, and free us to joyfully name, claim, and share the salvation we have received through Jesus' name. In Jesus' name we pray. Amen.

Words of Pardon

"God forgives our sin in Jesus' name, we've been born again in Jesus' name, and in Jesus' name I come to you, to share his love as he told me to." In the name of Jesus, you are forgiven. (Based on "Freely, Freely" from *The United Methodist Hymnal* [Nashville: The United Methodist Publishing House, 1989], no. 389.)

Benediction (Num. 6:24-26)

The LORD bless you and keep you;
the LORD make his face to shine upon you, and be gracious to you;
the LORD lift up his countenance upon you, and give you peace. Amen.
(May be spoken or sung.)

Epiphany

Barbara Shires Blaisdell

Isaiah 60: 1-6: Images of light, darkness, treasures, and journeys adorn this seasonal text. "Arise, shine, for your light has come. . . . "

Psalm 72: 1-7, 10-14: Prayers for the king are offered. He is a friend of the needy, a redeemer of the oppressed.

Ephesians 3:1-12: The "plan of the mystery hidden for ages in God" is revealed: the Gentiles have become "fellow heirs" of the gospel.

Matthew 2:1-12: The story of the wise men's journey to Bethlehem—and of what they found there.

REFLECTIONS

By common consent among most preachers, the Sunday after Christmas is the worst one of the year for preaching. Attendance is usually down. People are tired. There is an almost inevitable letdown from the rush and haste and happiness of Christmas. And there is also now more time for reflection. We have time to think about the little hurts that we suffered this season: the family member who was absent, the present that we got or gave that was really wrong, the things that didn't turn out the way we'd hoped. And preachers aren't immune to these hurts either. On top of all of this, there seems to be a certain letdown scripturally, too. Those soaring and ringing scripture texts of Advent—the ones from Isaiah telling of swords into plowshares, telling of "to us a son is born," telling of universal peace, angels, and goodwill to all—are behind us. Then finally, our culture is out of step with the Christian calendar—for most of us, the Christmas season stopped on Friday, and the next day the newspapers were full of after-Christmas sales and half-price gift wrap. But the church's calendar says that Christmas only began on Thursday, that this is the Christmas season right now, lasting for two more weeks. And if we are a bit tired, a bit disoriented, even a bit depressed, I think there's good reason for it.

For the question that the Sunday after Christmas confronts us with is this: How do we go back home to the normal routine, to our regular, mundane lives? And what shall we do when we get there?

A SERMON BRIEF

We are so familiar with the story of Epiphany, we have sung the song of the kings so many times, that we can fail to really hear the message, we can fail to ask questions of the story. We know, for instance, that the term "wise men" is the translation of a Greek word that means "magi." And in first-century Palestine, this was sort of a catchall term—it referred to magicians, astrologers, Zoroastrian priests, anyone, it seems, who hailed from "the East" and was interested in wisdom. The story tells us that they came to Bethlehem. They found Jesus. Then they left, and "returned home by another way." "They returned home by another way." A marvelous little phrase often overlooked in the story. But it camouflages a number of questions that I wish Matthew had spoken about more clearly: What did the wise men do when they got home? What difference had their visit made to them? Did they keep on reading the stars for signs? Did they keep on sifting entrails for prophecies? Were they changed? What happened? How did they return to the day-to-day routine after the great celebration?

I want to suggest three things that made their route home different, three things that changed their lives forever and completely, three things that they brought back from Bethlehem.

First of all, remember under whose sponsorship the wise men had come. This lovely story of the magi has its dark side, for the wise men came as agents of Herod. They had stopped in Jerusalem, and, in answer to Herod's question, they had said, "Sure, we'll tell you where the baby is." We know what Herod's intentions were. And I can't help thinking that those wise men, those magi, were wise enough to know that by accepting Herod's commission they themselves would be a party to Herod's great evil. And yet, they might have reasoned, "You have to go along to get along." "After all," they may have reasoned, "Herod's got the power. Let's not rock the boat. Sure, we'll tell you where that baby is."

And yet we know that they did not return to Herod. They did not carry out their commission to be Herod's spies. The scripture tells us, too cryptically, that they were "warned in a dream." But that's not enough. I think that they—and we—were prepared for that warning by what they had found there in Bethlehem.

What they had seen was this: that the real, ultimate, trustworthy, and moral power did not lie with the Herods of the world. No, the power was with God. And it was a God who came in the form of a baby, not in the uniform of a general. When you think about it, what is less powerful than a baby—and yet, paradoxically, what is more powerful to those of us who have ears to hear? For the cries of a baby—any baby—lure us to care. They call forth our energy and our concern. And that babe, lying there in that manger in Bethlehem, showed forth a God whose power lies precisely in the energy and concern and love that God can call forth from us. For that's the point of God coming as an infant. God's power is not coercive, not abusive. God's power is the power to provoke and call forth our care and concern and love. And having found that out, indeed, the wise men were changed. Indeed, they went home by another way, grasped by the power of what they had seen, lured by the loveliness of the ruler of the world.

There was a second thing that the wise men encountered during their holiday experience in Bethlehem. They were confronted with a vision of innocence, a God who holds forth innocence to us. Now I do not mean simply that they saw somebody—a baby—who hadn't had the opportunity to do anything awful yet. The reason that the church has traditionally wanted to maintain that Jesus Christ was innocent, was sinless, is not because anyone knows that for an absolute fact. Even if someone did, that's not the point. The point is that, in Jesus, those wise men are confronted with newness. And it was not the newness of a God who has decided to give up and make a completely original start. No, what the wise men saw was the God who comes to them, to you and me, with newness in every single moment. The God who comes with possibility. The God who comes afresh into every life in every moment.

The wise men went to Bethlehem simply curious about one more celestial novelty. They went to Bethlehem playing footsie with Herod. They went to Bethlehem cynical and jaded. "But they returned home by another way." They saw and they heard that God comes, come what may, afresh and energizing in every moment. They saw in that baby a God who is not completely constrained by what has been. They saw a God who comes to make you and me into "new creations," as Paul says. And so, indeed, "they returned home by another way."

And those wise men saw a final thing at that lowly stable, for power and innocence alone would not have been enough to cause their hearts to take a detour home. They also saw hope in that God who revealed Godself in the form of a baby. Now the wise men were probably endowed with about as much hope as any other people. They hoped that their camels wouldn't break a leg. They hoped that their water would last. They hoped that the gifts that they had brought to Bethlehem hadn't fractured the credit limit on their Master Cards—the same sort of garden-variety hopes that you or I have. But in Bethlehem they were confronted with hope on a breathtaking scale. They were confronted with a hope that, as Matthew tells the story, made their trip—which had been undertaken simply out of curiosity—into an experience of worship. For they were confronted with the hope of God for humanity, for creation, for them, for you and me. There in that animal stall they were confronted with a God whose hope is not of the garden-variety kind. They were confronted with the news of a God who could feel all of the pain of a too-often sorry world, and still have hope for that world. They were met by a God who is not blind, who knows the world in all its awfulness and terror, and yet who does not give up—now or ever.

And so, "they returned home by another way." They were changed. No longer could they be the instruments of a government of oppression. No longer could they repose in cynicism. No longer could they face the world with mere curiosity about its sometimes strange doings, holding themselves removed and aloof from the cries of all babies and children everywhere. No, they were changed, I think. For they had been confronted, those wise men, with the power and the newness and the hope of God for them and for all creatures.

Their story is our story too, I think. Home by a different way, never to be the same again. For God has come to us. In hope and in power, forever and ever. So, now, even as the tree is consigned to a box or Dumpster, even as the gift wrappings grace the inside of a bag instead of the outside of a box, even as all the batteries go dead—know that God's tenderness is offered to you now and always, know that the Lord is love unfailing, know that the hope of God is eternal, know that Christmas has come. And so we too, you and I, can go home by a different way. The journey awaits us. Amen.

SUGGESTIONS FOR WORSHIP

Call to Worship (Isa. 60:1-6 adapted)

LEADER: Arise, shine for your light has come.

PEOPLE: **Nations shall come to the light, and rulers shall be drawn by its brightness.**

LEADER: Lift up your eyes and look around; your sons shall come from afar and your daughters shall be carried in their nannies' arms.

PEOPLE: **Then shall all see and be glad.**

ALL: **Then shall all proclaim the praise of the Lord.**

Prayer of Confession

Gracious God, you are slow to anger and abounding in steadfast love, but we have tested your limits. We are slow to forgive, slow to include, slow to yield to your lure. We are abounding in fear and steadfast in pride. Forgive us and turn us, O God. Fill our minds with your light and our hearts with your love. In Jesus' name. Amen.

Assurance of Pardon

If we walk in the light, as God is in the light, we have fellowship with one another, and the blood of Jesus Christ, God's Son, cleanses us from all sin (I John 1:7 adapted).
Friends, believe the Good News. In Jesus Christ we are forgiven.

Benediction

In former generations, the mystery was not made known to human
    kind.
But now it has been revealed by the Spirit:
That is, that we have all become fellow heirs
    and sharers of the promise—in Jesus Christ.
So that through the church, the wisdom of God—
    in all its rich variety—might be made known.
So, then—
Go out into the world in peace
As sharers of the promise
Witnesses of God's wild, wondrous ways,
Bearers of God's love.

First Sunday After Epiphany (Baptism of the Lord)

Gail McDougle

Isaiah 43:1-7: Isaiah utters the reassuring promise of God, calling to mind God's presence with Israel even "should you pass through the sea." Israel is reminded of its Exodus crossing in waters full of threat, which proved to be a river that flowed toward freedom. Isaiah says God is about to do a similar thing for the nation in captivity.

Psalm 29: The psalm is a celebration of God's voice heard and experienced in the power of storm. God is in the wind, the rain, the lightning. The psalmist assures us that God is enthroned over the storm, even when it becomes a threatening flood.

Acts 8: Philip's ministry of accompanying and explaining ends with the Ethiopian eunuch's baptism. The author of Acts makes clear the connection of the Christian proclamation of Jesus as Messiah with the practice of Christian baptism to all, even the servant of an African monarch.

Luke 3:15-17, 21-22: Jesus is baptized in the Jordan by John, and a heavenly voice is heard, saying, "You are my Son, the Beloved; with you I am well pleased."

REFLECTIONS

The challenge of this Sunday is finding a new insight to explore in an event of Jesus' life that is familiar to most worshipers. Whether they know Luke's version per se, most certainly know the story: John is baptizing in the Jordan;

people question whether he is the Messiah; John insists a Greater One is coming; Jesus appears and receives John's baptism; a heavenly voice speaks and the Spirit appears as a dove.

Poised just before Jesus' public ministry and charged with no less a voice than God's, the story is certainly imbued with power and importance. It is one of only two places in Luke's Gospel where "that" voice is heard. The other (the Transfiguration in 9:28-36) like this one delivers a very similar message: "This is my Son, my Chosen; listen to him!"

What was the intended impact of these similar messages? Is this told as a simple straightforward claim God makes about Jesus heard by those present? Sitting where it does in Luke, how is it related to the public ministry that ensued? Was the voice's message a revelation only to those who heard it, or was it a revelation to Jesus, too?

Rarely is the latter purported. Yet it makes more sense of what follows— namely, Jesus' embracing, inclusive, compassionate ministry. Standing there in Jordan's muddy water, did Jesus catch sight of God's essential truth: that every son or daughter is God's son or daughter, and all are beloved? Was that revelation what fueled his remarkable ministry?

A Sermon Brief

All four of the New Testament Gospels give an account of Jesus' baptism in the Jordan. Interestingly, Luke, whose narrative is usually the most graceful, dramatic, and complete of the four Gospels, offers the most clumsy, undynamic, and sparse telling of this pivotal moment in Jesus' life.

Still, as clumsily as Luke tells it, the event is imbued with some remarkable phenomena: God speaks and Luke quotes God verbatim. The heavens open. A dove descends. Certainly, this is not normal fare for a muddy Jordan River baptism by John, the wild man in camel skin. This certainly is not what had been happening as hundreds of desperate, needy peasants came to him for baptism . . . hoping for something to change their lot in life . . . hoping that this fierce holy man's baptism might prepare the way for a different order . . . hoping that their submission to ritual cleansing might set in motion a powerful change in the way things were.

Is that what brought Jesus there, one among many? We do not know. Luke does not tell us. The text is silent. All that Luke tells us about Jesus' state of mind is that Jesus was prayerful. Again he does not tell us the focus of his prayers. But Jesus comes for John's baptism, likely with the Baptizer's sense that God was about to do something powerful.

In the Baptizer's message, there was a sense of expectancy, even if the human chances seemed slim to none. The Baptizer kept proclaiming one far more powerful than he who would reconstruct things on earth, who would sort it all out, who would separate the wheat from the chaff and the wonderful from the sordid and the fair from the unjust. John, the Baptizer, proclaimed that such a one was overdue and perhaps might even be on his way.

Why did Jesus come? What did he hope to happen? What was his baptism by John supposed to accomplish? Was there something in the water? We do not know. The text does not say. The text is silent.

But the heavens are not silent! They open, but are not turbulent. They speak, but do not thunder. They affirm, and do not condemn. They do not pour down and drown the Galilean in the Jordan's muddy water.

Exactly what happened to Jesus in his depths with the muddy Jordan water rushing round him, we do not know. The text does not say. The text, for the moment, is silent. But whatever happened, Luke would have us believe, was formative, decisive, life-changing.

Luke uses a very particular verb: he says Jesus "turned" from the Jordan. It was a turning point. Things would never be the same: Jesus left the Jordan, "full of the Holy Spirit," Luke says.

But what was the baptism for, what about? How can we find out? Luke doesn't explain, doesn't lay it out for us. For that matter, neither do the other Gospel writers. But, by what followed, we know that the baptism was important and pivotal. Jesus' life was never again the same.

It was not back to Nazareth and carpentry and business as usual, but to the desert and struggle and centering, and to constant motion and constant reaching out to the miserable ones. It was to reaching out even to the comfortable ones whose misery was only less apparent, because they wore the socially and culturally acceptable masks of self-righteousness, apathy, superiority, and civility.

It was not back to carpentry in Nazareth where a decent job provided basic security and three squares a day. No, not back to carpentry and Nazareth, but to being out there, on the road, building something in and with people—the "kingdom of God," he called it—where God's reign coming in brought people together around tables of acceptance no matter who they were or what they had done or failed to do.

It was not back to carpentry, but to building something in and with people. Something built by gracious, compassionate touch—eyes, skin, arms, legs, hearts. It was the kingdom coming to broken, withered, wild bodies, and broken, poisoned, lost spirits.

It was not back to isolation, anonymity, carpentry in Nazareth, but to presence, popularity, and power, building something graceful and just in and with people: the kingdom coming, changing lives and the world forever.

The Jordan River water may have been murky. The Heavenly Voice was not. It was in the open, clear, so clear it was quotable: "You are my Son, the Beloved; with you I am well pleased."

That's Luke's only clue. It wasn't the water. It was the words, the affirmation, the revelation that caused the turning, centered the focus of his life, and fueled the compassion that changed the world. Whatever limiting, shackling, partial understanding Jesus brought to the Jordan was washed away in the water by the words of unconditional acceptance and delight Jesus heard from the heart of God. And he must have understood they were and still are the words every human heart hungers to hear: "You are God's child. God takes delight in you, just as you are, just now."

It was not back to carpentry in Nazareth, but out among the desperate and lost people, hungering to hear that Good News. The message that changed Jesus' life forever still has the gentle, transforming power to change ours.

SUGGESTIONS FOR WORSHIP

Call to Worship

LEADER: As Jesus stood in Jordan's muddy waters,

PEOPLE: **We come with all the unclear and muddy things
in our life to worship God.**

LEADER: As Jesus submitted to John's baptism,

PEOPLE: **We would submit our lives to love's transforming touch.**

LEADER: As Jesus trusted God's spirit to wash over him,

PEOPLE: **We would trust God's spirit to wash away our sins and fears.**

LEADER: As Jesus left the Jordan to give his life to God,

PEOPLE: **So we would leave here today with a renewed sense of God's
presence in our lives.**

ALL: **We bring ourselves,
Wanting to be daughters and sons
In whom God takes delight.
We come to worship God!**

Renewal of Baptismal Vow

O God, my God,

I bring myself once more to claim the gentle power of my baptism. I open myself again to the grace of your love, so that I might become what you would have me be. Amen.

Prayer of Dedication

Each time we bring our gifts to you, O God, we would bring ourselves as well. Like Jesus at the Jordan, we would open ourselves to your revelation for our lives, to your call to love and serve. Admiring and remembering Jesus, we pray. Amen.

Ash Wednesday

Patricia A. Spearman

Isaiah 58:1-12: God respects sacrifice that is given from the heart as opposed to that which is done for tradition's sake. When we bring our offerings, they should be given with pure motives. This scripture reminds us that indeed it is our *walk* not our *talk* that shows the world we are children of the most high God.

Psalm 51:1-17: The psalmist begins by recognizing his shortcomings and making a request to God for total forgiveness and restoration. The soliloquy represents metanoia coming from the depths of his heart.

II Corinthians 5:20b–6:10: The writer brings the paradox of salvation before the church at Corinth by saying, in effect: "When it appears we have nothing, we have everything through Christ." There are overtones here of Acts 2:44. Within the community of believers, the freedom to share minimizes the burden of need, the writer believes. As someone once said, "We may not have it altogether, but together we can have it all." We "re-present" God through our willingness to "freely" give grace to others just as we have freely received it.

Matthew 6:1-6, 16-21: Jesus speaks here to those who see righteous living as an item on their personal resume. Our gifts must be made with sincerity of heart. The real blessing comes as God recognizes our endeavors, not through the accolades of human beings.

REFLECTIONS

In our society today, we tend to relish the new and discount the old. We have established a tradition of a new car every three to four years, new clothes to fit special occasions, and, depending on the time of year, new makeup to match the season. Psalm 51 gives a calculated approach to discovering the relevance of "newness" as its relates to our relationship with God and growth in our Christian walk.

As much as we pretend to be "all right," the truth is that we have all sinned and come short of God's divine purpose for our lives. We have learned to use *sin* as a mystical scapegoat for these shortcomings. In reality, it is our free will/choice that plunges us into the depths of brokenness. Most of us don't have the slightest notion of the meaning of the word "sin." I grew up in a fundamentalist church setting. I could recite the sins of the world on command: (1) Don't cheat on your spouse; (2) Don't drink; (3) Don't smoke; (4) Don't dance; (5) Don't listen to rock and roll music; (6) Women don't wear pants; and so forth. I was so busy memorizing all of the "don'ts," I did not take time to understand what I should do for Christian growth.

In retrospect, I see now that sin is not something defined by an action; rather, it grows out of the intent of the heart.

The confession of David in this psalm clearly speaks of a sin that took him out of his relationship with God and the community. His request for God's mercy, a clean heart, and a new spirit suggest that his sin devastated more than his physical temple. Indeed, there was damage to his soul. Such a prayer as his is difficult to pray because it requires self-examination. We're very good at examining others, but it can be painful to look at our own selves.

I am always amazed at the number of deaths from breast cancer that are classified as preventable, if only the woman had done monthly self-examinations. I've asked some patients going through radiation if they had complied with medical wisdom on a monthly basis. Usually the answer is the same: "I was afraid I might find something wrong." This is indeed an irony, because the purpose of the examination is to prevent a small problem from becoming a bigger one with fatal consequences. Before my brothers get too cozy with this analogy, the scenario is the same when it comes to their noticing symptoms of prostate cancer and regularly obtaining prostate examinations. Regardless of the gender, we as human beings usually shirk the responsibility of self-examination. We allow the fear of finding something to paralyze us. Ignoring a problem doesn't make it go away!

There are some things that require a view from the outside, but our personal walk with God requires a view from the inside out. As uncomfortable as it may be, "self-examination" is a critical ingredient for Christian growth.

A SERMON BRIEF

One of the most difficult things I must overcome constantly is the preparation phase of preaching a sermon. Once I've decided on a text, completed the word study, and tried to look at the present-day implications, I always find a mirror staring at me through my word processor. No matter how hard I may try to escape the personal implications of the text, I am forced to see the message from God as the light shines on me. There have been times I've begun work on a text thinking, "I sure hope Sister Sally and Brother Bubba are at church. They really need to hear this." Before I get too cocky, I feel a sting with the realization that some of the contents of this dynamite message have my name written all over them. Sometimes this reality check comes midweek, but more often it happens right in the middle of Sunday morning delivery. To add insult to injury, I look at the congregation and see that Sister Sally and Brother Bubba aren't even there! Talk about uncomfortable. It makes me warm around the collar. If I have to get chastised, I want the other culprits to have their fair share of the spanking.

As a child, I was the prankster in my family. I invented ways to upset my siblings, irritate my parents, and get others in trouble while keeping my hands clean. It wasn't long before my mom and dad figured out if trouble was brewing, I was somewhere with the spoon in my hand. Even if I didn't instigate the problem, many times I was chastised with everyone else. The caveat statement was, "If you didn't do this, I know there is something else you've done and *thought* you got away with." Needless to say, I would always take on the victim's mentality and wonder why they wanted to pick on me. The truth is, there were some things I'd been guilty of and for which I'd never received appropriate discipline.

I smile when I look back on those days. I knew when I was doing something I should not do. I knew when I neglected to do something I should have done. My problem was facing my responsibility in the punishment phase. I wanted the laughs that came with the prank, but I didn't want the chastisement after the fact. Our family was rather large, so anytime someone got spanked, there were plenty of mouths to tell the story to the whole neighborhood. I'd usually try to avoid my friends for several days after being punished. Come to think of it, I'd try to avoid my siblings and myself, too. Getting caught was bad enough; accepting the consequences for my actions doubled the pain.

I resonate with David's plea for mercy. You see, even though I've had more than thirty years in the church, there are still some areas that need improvement. I've had to look at myself *after* losing my temper. I've had to look at myself *after* saying an unkind word. I've had to look at myself *after* a bitter or vindictive thought. Friends, I really didn't like the picture in the mirror. My initial instinct was to do as I did when I was a child—run away and hide from the world. I hear the words of David very clearly during those times of personal pain. More important, the love that God has shown, in the person of Jesus Christ, continues to speak volumes to my disconsolate soul. It was during those times that I realized just how much I really needed God's presence. For you see, I was forced to go through a personal examination. The fear of finding something was muted by the knowledge that God was still with me. The perplexing dilemma of self-examination was eased by the knowledge that God was still working on me. I found a quiet comfort shouting through the "dark of my soul," saying, "I'm with you to provide just what you need. My grace is sufficient for you."

There have been times in my life when I couldn't go to anyone with my "True Confession." I turned to God, who has always been faithful to hear, forgive, and heal. As we prepare for the joy of Easter, let's not forget the perilous journey of Lent. This is a time for necessary self-examination. I'll be so busy looking at myself, I may not have time to identify your faults. I promise you one thing, my sisters and brothers. When we complete this process, we'll all repeat the chorus found in verse 10 of the text: "Create in me a clean heart and renew a right spirit." Amen.

SUGGESTIONS FOR WORSHIP

Call to Worship

LEADER: It is by the goodness of God that we have another opportunity to gather.

PEOPLE: **If it had not been for the Lord on our side, we would have perished long ago.**

LEADER: For all that the Lord has done for us . . . Is there anything you want to say?

PEOPLE: **Yes, we want to say, "Thank you, Lord."**

LEADER: For the continual blessings in our lives . . . Is there anything you want to say?

PEOPLE: **Yes, we want to say, "Thank you, Lord."**

LEADER: The God who creates, heals, restores, and gives us joy has been *very* good to us. Is there a tangible offering you want to give the Lord?

PEOPLE: **Yes! We bring now our offering of praise into this sanctuary. We bring our lives, minds, and bodies to this worship experience. We are ready to give our all to you, Lord.**

LEADER: In this house on this day, let us invite the Light of the World to be ever present with us.

ALL: **Shine, Lord. Shine in us. Shine through us. Light our lives and this house with your presence. Shine, Lord! Shine!**

Prayer of Confession

Lord, we like sheep have gone astray. We have become conceited in the gifts that you gave to us. We fail many times to give you the glory for your continued blessings. We use our traditions as a measure of piety. We have sinned and come short of your design for our lives. We ask, now, O Lord, that you forgive us. Turn your light on our souls. Wash us, cleanse us, and give us, once again, your spirit of truth, sincerity, and love. We want to represent you to the world, so that all will know of your grace, mercy, and peace. Amen.

Assurance of Pardon

As a mother caresses her tearful child and a father loves all of his children, so God is faithful, loving, and forgiving to all who come with a repentant spirit. In the name of God the creator and the God of wisdom, you are forgiven.

Sending Forth

Lord, we gather to praise your name. You blessed us through the praise. We leave this Lighthouse to go into a world that is filled with darkness. Let us be a beacon of light. . . . This little light of mine. I must let it shine!

Second Sunday in Lent

Lucy Lind Hogan

Genesis 15:1-12, 17-18: Having made our commitment to God there still come moments when we question God's faithfulness. This passage is about Abram's uncertainty and God's certainty. When, in a vision, God came to Abram to reassure him that the covenant was still in place, Abram challenged God. "How am I going to know that what you are saying is true? Give me a sign!" Just as it was good news for Abram that God respected Abram's challenge and gave him signs—the stars, the smoking fire pot, and the flaming torch—it is also good news for us. God is faithful.

Psalm 27: The psalmist realizes that when we find ourselves in difficult and dangerous situations our confidence fades. We may know intellectually that God is the stronghold of our lives, but in the midst of the assaults of our enemies we need to be reassured of God's presence. A glimpse of God's loving face will strengthen our fainting hearts.

Philippians 3:17–4:1: The truth of Paul's observations about human nature is undimmed by the passage of time. How many people do we know whose lives are destined surely for self-destruction? Paul does not necessarily preach that Christians who dedicate their lives to God are superior as much as he proclaims that, by following Jesus Christ, we will "choose life" so that we and our descendants will live.

Luke 13:31-35: Jesus' lament over Jerusalem.

REFLECTIONS

The events of the Passion and the Cross should be no surprise to anyone reading Luke's Gospel, for scattered throughout the text are allusions to those events. In this brief passage alone are the declarations that Herod wants to kill Jesus, that a prophet must be killed in Jerusalem, and that Jesus is firmly resolved to go to Jerusalem. The preacher may wish to focus on the strong christological statement made by this passage, that Jesus was the prophet/Messiah sent from God of whom the prophecies had spoken. The preacher may also choose to focus on the image of God as a mother hen. How interesting that in the midst of these harsh predictions of suffering and death is found such loving, nurturing concern. This also foreshadows the concern of Jesus on the cross for his mother and the crucified thief. Luke witnesses to the truth that even though Jerusalem (i.e., humanity) was responsible for putting its Messiah to death, God promised to remain steadfast and loving, slow to anger, and abounding in great mercy.

A SERMON BRIEF

When I was younger, much to my parents' chagrin, I loved *MAD* magazine. I particularly enjoyed a recurring cartoon about the revealing nature of shadows. A scene would be played out in front of a wall. The format was simple—a drawing of a young woman accepting a gift from her date. But the shadows on the wall behind them would reveal what the young woman was *really* thinking. The real young woman was grateful for the small gift, but the even more "real" shadow young woman would be running away crying, hurt that her date would even think of giving her such a small gift.

I now suspect that I was attracted to that cartoon because I recognized that we all play shadow games. There are so many times when our shadow would like to tell the truth and show our anger, but our real self knows that anger and truth may be hurtful, or counterproductive, or even dangerous.

When confronted with an injustice, has your shadow had the courage to be like Jesus, thumbing your nose at those in power, calling them names, and carrying on with the ministry of justice in spite of their resistance? But has the real you been a Pharisee? Were you so conscious of the dangerous situation in which your words and actions were going to place you, that you decided it was wise to play it safe?

I wonder if that well-intentioned group of Pharisees actually went to Herod and delivered Jesus' message? This group of Pharisees, usually portrayed as the enemy is, in this brief encounter *seemingly* trying to do Jesus a favor. Luke tells us that a crowd of thousands was listening to Jesus (Luke 12:1). If one reviews his statements to the crowd, one is confronted with a startling series of disturbing pronouncements: "I came to bring fire to the earth" (Luke 12:49a); "Do you think that I have come to bring peace to the earth? No, I tell you, but rather division!" (Luke 12:51); and the lesson that we will read next week, "I tell you; but unless you repent, you will all perish" (Luke 13:5). It is understandable that one might wish to caution Jesus that his remarks are inflammatory and likely to incur the wrath of the authorities, but I suspect their words of warning were dripping with irony.

An inescapable reality of life is that people will not always agree or come easily and quickly to a consensus. When there is disagreement, there is great potential for conflict and confrontation. Conflict and confrontation are, at the heart, about power and control. They arise when people seek to find resolution to their disagreements and power struggles. Confrontation is everywhere, and a look at the newspaper, or in our own homes and churches, tells us that we don't always handle conflict very well.

Nevertheless, times are sure to arise when, as Paul reminds us, we must "stand firm in the Lord," to confront and challenge those who are "enemies of the cross of Christ." We are daily presented with a dilemma. How can we be faithful prophets who passionately, yet compassionately, become the voice of God's justice and grace in the world? How are we to harmonize our real selves with our shadows? What are our options, anger and violence, or retreat and silence? Or, are there better, more constructive ways of handling conflict and disagreement? Are there loving ways to respect the other while asserting one's identity as a valued child of God? How can we harmonize our real selves with our shadow selves?

Lent is a time of reflection and reform when we review our relationship with God and with others and prepare to celebrate resurrection, the gift of new life that is possible for all of God's creatures. The lessons chosen for the second Sunday in Lent challenge us to rethink the ways we assert ourselves— before God and the world. They are lessons about conflict and confrontation.

Jesus confronted the worldly powers that sought to silence him and his message of life and hope. This brief passage is an interesting mixture of bold and fearless assertiveness, prophetic proclamation, and pastoral concern. I would suggest that in this combination we find a model for Christian confrontation.

To stand firm in the Lord and confront the enemies of the Cross requires a fearless assertiveness. Jesus was not dissuaded by Herod's threat, and in fact, he boldly challenged the Pharisees to deliver a message from Jesus to "that fox."

Many of us are not comfortable with such bold assertiveness. We have been socialized to be polite and indirect. We want to make our point and stand firm, but we also do not want to anger or insult even our opponents.

Fortunately, the pages of the history of the church are filled with the stories of countless women and men who stood firm before those who would silence them, some even to the point of death.

While most of us will not be called upon to give our lives for our faith, there will be times when God calls us to be fearlessly assertive. A seminary classmate and friend recently found herself in such a situation. Jane Dixon is a suffragan (assisting) bishop in the Episcopal Church. In the twenty years since the Episcopal Church voted to ordain women deacons, priests, and bishops, enormous change has taken place. Ten percent of Episcopal clergy are now women. However, a few bishops remain who will not ordain women or accept them into their dioceses. And there are individual churches that will not accept ordained women. After years of being told to go slowly and not to force congregations to accept the visitation of a female bishop, Ronald Haines, the bishop of Washington, under whom my friend serves, decided that the time had come when he would no longer allow any congregations in the diocese of Washington to reject Bishop Dixon.

On a cold, snowy Sunday in January, Jane arrived at St. Luke's Church to begin her visitation. The emotional temperature in the church matched the actual temperature outside. Only three of the congregation's parishioners were present. Silent and unsmiling, they sat in the back pew "as observers." No candle glow warmed the winter morning. The candlesticks, chalice, and paten had all been removed from the church.

To this difficult worship service Jane brought bread and wine from the cathedral. She brought a congregation—several friends—to warm the cold church. But most important like Jesus before her, she brought the strength of God's message that all people—women and men—are created in the image of God. Jane brought the love of God and compassion for those who were still struggling to understand the ramifications of this truth.

Eventually seven members of St. Luke's, one of whom also brought bread and wine to be used, came to join the visitors who were worshiping in their church. Marie Warren, a member of the congregation, said she and her husband came "in an effort to bring about peace in this conflict of ideals" (Debbi Wilgoren, "Episcopal Parish Shuns Mass by a Visiting Female Bishop," *Washington Post*, 15 January, 1996, B4).

Coming in peace, with the Good News of God's reconciling justice and love, Bishop Dixon and those who accompanied her went out to confront those who had rejected their message. They reached out in love to those who, like the Pharisees, urged them to go slowly and to temper their message. They stood firm in their convictions.

Christian confrontation for the sake of the gospel means bringing release to the captives. We are called to bring healing and wholeness to a troubled world and that means being in the thick of things. As Christians we do not run away or bring the Good News from a distance. Rather, we must be willing to risk our lives, our reputations, all we have. Our shadow self and our real self must be one.

But we must also recognize that Jesus' confrontation also included compassion and concern. His words of justice and judgment also included the good news of God's love and forgiveness. Jesus' prophecy for Jerusalem included the tender and loving image of God who accepts us as a loving mother hen who "gathers her brood under her wings."

As Christians we are confronted daily with situations of conflict and hostility. We are called upon not to rise up with anger. Rather, we are called upon to face boldly and fearlessly those who do wrong, confident in the knowledge that God would have us bring a word of love and healing into the midst of the conflict, and grounded in the knowledge and security of a God who loves us first.

SUGGESTIONS FOR WORSHIP

Call to Worship

LEADER: We praise you, O Holy One, who created the water and the dry land.

PEOPLE: **We sing praises to you, our loving God, who created all the peoples of the earth. We truly are as many as the stars in heaven.**

LEADER: We come together seeking your comfort and direction.

PEOPLE: **Gather us under your wing, gentle and tender one.**

LEADER: Teach us your ways,

PEOPLE: **And give us the courage to confront the evil that surrounds us.**

Prayer of Confession

Holy God, you are always more ready to listen than we are to pray. Hear us as we come before you opening our hearts and minds to your loving and gracious judgment. We lay before you our arrogance and selfishness. But most of all we confess our lack of trust in your devotion and constancy. Day after day we listen to the voices of the world urging divisiveness, hatred, and bitterness, while we ignore the words of truth and justice spoken by your faithful servants. Forgive us, and fill us with your spirit of hope that we may become signs of reconciling light and love. All this we ask in the name of your love incarnate, the light of the world, Jesus. Amen.

Words of Assurance

Hear the good news, we are the children of Abraham and Sarah, the children of a loving and faithful God who forgives us, now and forever.

Sending Forth

God calls us into the world to be reconciling light and love. Stand firm in the strength of God, constant in love, and dedicated always to God's faithful service.

Third Sunday in Lent

Lucy Lind Hogan

Isaiah 55:1-9: Israel was nearing a crucial turning point in its corporate life. Years of pain, sorrow, and separation were apparently soon to come to an end. Exile would be replaced by feasting and celebration. The prophet assures the people of God that they have not been forgotten or abandoned.

Psalm 63:1-8: The psalm continues the images of nourishment and abundance. The dryness of the soul without God is contrasted with rich feast available to all who will call upon God's name.

I Corinthians 10:1-13: The Corinthians are exorted not to give into temptation as the Israelites did during their desert wanderings. Though no one is immune to temptation, Paul says, "God will not let you be tempted beyond your strength."

Luke 13:1-9: The parable of the fig tree: Jesus challenges his listeners to be accountable for the way they live their lives.

REFLECTIONS

Repentance and death are certainly themes that reverberate throughout the Lenten season. Today's Gospel lesson speaks to both. The parable of the fig tree can serve as a call for individuals to examine their fruitfulness, and/or the parable can draw the church and the larger society into an examination of its collective conscience. One might also read Luke's interpretation of the parable as a condemnation of the people of Israel. The ax was shortly to be laid to the root. But in any case, Christians should not get smug; daily the church is confronted with the "fruit" of its barrenness. Similarly, today's Epistle lesson warns believers against becoming overconfident.

Recently an automobile manufacturer, so certain of its product, claimed that it would pay a huge sum of money if an accident in its air-bag-equipped car proved fatal. Daily we put our trust in any number of products. Paul is writing about trust in God—or more precisely, our loss of memory and lack of trust. Do not, he urges, be like the Israelites who were fed and nourished by God, only to forget who kept them safe. We humans prefer to put our trust in golden calves and air bags, things we can see and touch. Paul reminds us that in difficult times it is God, not calves or air bags, that will save us.

A Sermon Brief

The morning was a normal, hectic, frantic Friday. The rush that morning was compounded by the fact that I was leaving on a business trip later in the morning and had to make sure that everything was prepared. In the midst of the controlled chaos I heard my husband's anxious voice quietly, yet firmly asking me to come upstairs. Immediately I knew that something was wrong.

With a knot in my stomach I climbed the stairs where I was met by my husband and my sobbing ten-year-old son. When my son had gone in to check on the newest addition to our family, a two-month-old hamster, he had found Sapphire dead. The small hamster's neck had been broken accidentally by the exercise wheel.

Suddenly my son was confronted with the reality of mortality. He knew that people died. Within the span of a year he had lost two family members. But this was a small, dependent being that he had nurtured, and fed, and kept safe and warm. Sapphire was his responsibility, and he had fulfilled his responsibility admirably.

Suddenly everything had changed. His new friend was dead and my son was confronted by a cascade of questions for which he had no answers. Why had this happened? What had he done wrong? Was he responsible? Did God do this? I felt as helpless as he did. I was sickened by the death, anxious about his feelings, but I had to go to the seminary to teach an 8:30 class, and he had to get to school. Fortunately his father, while driving him to school, spoke to him about his feelings, and acknowledged the questions that we all have when someone or something dies. Together they began to explore God's role in both our lives and our deaths.

Daily we all are confronted by the truth that "in the midst of life we are in death." The newspaper may chill us with the news of one more death by accident, murder, or war. Or it may be the phone call we dread that tells us someone we love has died. The reality of death constantly intrudes into all of our activities and our relationships. When death overshadows our lives, we seek answers to the questions that weigh heavily on our hearts. Why is there suffering and death? How are we to live when daily confronted by suffering and death?

Shortly after Sapphire's untimely death a new hamster occupied the cage—minus the exercise wheel. SJ (Sapphire Junior) helped my son understand the difficult lesson that life must go on. Unfortunately our questions are not as easily relieved as buying a new hamster.

In his Gospel account Luke records an exchange between Jesus and a group of people who reported to Jesus that Pilate had executed a group of Galileans. An assumption was left unspoken; suffering and death are the result of sin. Those executed by Pilate must have been notorious sinners. We can almost hear the smugness in their voices: "Since we are not notorious sinners, we will be safe." We are no different from that group that confronted Jesus. All too often we sidestep the difficult questions raised by death and suffering by convincing ourselves that bad things happen to bad people, good things happen to good people, and that is the will of God.

Unfortunately, Jesus did not respond with words of comfort and agreement. Instead, he reminded his interrogators about the tower of Siloam and the eighteen people who were killed when it fell. Was their accidental death also a result of their sin, he asked? Sinners die, everyone dies, he declares. Just as the rain falls on the just and unjust, so too does death. Jesus reminds us of the fact that "in the midst of life we are in death." Death will come, sometimes sooner, sometimes later, but it will come. This is the reality with which we all must cope. By the very act of breathing we are constantly in peril. To be alive means to be confronted with death.

Jesus does not offer us an escape from death. Jesus challenges us to live life fully even while fully acknowledging our mortality. Rather than fixating on the end time, we should be daily focused on the life that we have been given and how we live that life. Repent. Turn your life around. Live your life as though you could lose it at any moment, because you could.

I think that moment came home most forcefully to me and to my family when my husband was diagnosed with cancer. In one swift moment our world came crashing down around us, and we knew things would never be the same again. Fortunately, because his cancer was caught early, my husband is healthy and well nine years later. But we came to understand what it means to live in the valley of the shadow of death.

For some this knowledge brings reckless abandonment: eat, drink, and be merry, for tomorrow we die. Others withdraw from the world overwhelmed by the apparent futility of it all. What is God calling us to do? To help us understand, Jesus tells the story of a gardener who hoped to rescue a barren fig tree. His imagery is not too subtle: we are the fig tree, God is the owner, Jesus is the gardener.

The public works department where I live periodically drives through the streets identifying trees that need to be trimmed or removed. They spray paint the trunks with different colors indicating to the work crews that will follow the fates of the different trees. Blue tells them to trim the limbs. Bright orange means cut the tree down; it is hopeless.

Jesus confronts us with the knowledge that we all should be wearing a bright orange mark. We have been neglecting our call from God to bear fruit, and because of that we all deserve to be cut down. Our barrenness manifests itself in our separation from one another, our violence, our lack of compassion and concern, and our self-centered preoccupation.

Jesus' word of judgment is quickly followed by a word of forgiveness and hope. In spite of our bright orange mark we all have been given chance after chance to bear fruit—but we must be properly cultivated and adequately fertilized. The compassionate gardener assured the owner of the vineyard that he would "dig around the tree and put manure on it."

We must repent, Jesus tells us. But how does one cultivate and fertilize one's soul? Most of us now live lives far removed from fig trees, pruning, and manure. What perhaps seemed apparent to Jesus' audience is lost on urban dwellers.

I grew up in a city where my gardening consisted of transplanting geraniums and petunias and weeding my grandparents' shrubbery bed. You can imagine how surprised I was when I moved to Iowa after I was married. When I hear Jesus talk about fertilizing the fig tree, I cannot help recalling my Iowan mother-in-law and her tomato plants. Although she had moved into an apartment, Clarissa made sure that each spring she planted a few tomato plants by the back door. She carefully tended her plants, but I was always skeptical of her unorthodox method of fertilizing them. She never bothered with products from the nursery. No, each morning Clarissa would pour leftover coffee over the plants. Then she would sprinkle the soil with coffee grounds, eggshells, and banana peels. Unorthodox, perhaps. Effective, definitely. My skepticism would last only until I bit into the biggest, juiciest, sweetest tomato I had ever tasted.

My mother-in-law tended her plants with love and daily attention. We will never bear fruit until we cultivate and fertilize our souls with the same love and daily attention. But what is the spiritual equivalent of coffee grounds and eggshells? Are we disrespectful if we think of daily Bible study as manure for the soul? I think that the tears of joy and pain we shed together in corporate worship water our spirits. And we cultivate our souls by attending to acts of justice and compassion that break up the hard soil that forms around our hearts. Then, with the help of the Gardener, we will bear sweet, juicy fruit.

The fruit borne by a well-tended soul will not prevent our death. Ultimately we all must confront the certainty of our death and the death of all that we know and love. Yes, in the midst of life we are in death. But Jesus calls us to live that life fully, cultivating and nurturing our souls with daily care and attention. Isaiah and Jesus both remind us that, if we will but return to the God who created us and loves us, we will have life and will have it abundantly.

Suggestions for Worship

Call to Worship

LEADER: You who thirst, come to the living water.

PEOPLE: **You who hunger after righteousness and truth, come to the living God.**

LEADER: Come and worship our God who spreads a table before us,

PEOPLE: **A table overflowing with milk and honey.**

LEADER: Sing praises to God for the bread of life,

PEOPLE: **Eat what is good, and delight in the rich food of God's gracious love.**

LEADER: Give thanks to our God whose way is abundant mercy.

PEOPLE: **Rejoice, for God will pardon all who return.**

Prayer of Confession

Holy One of Israel, have compassion on us as we wander through the wilderness of life. We turn our eyes from the pillars of cloud and fire that you send to give us direction. Our mouths are dry, thirsting for your living water. Our bodies ache with hunger, longing for the food of your word. Pour out your abundant grace upon all who are gathered here. Cultivate and nourish our souls that we may once again turn and walk in your ways. All this we ask in the name of the one who is life itself, Jesus the Christ. Amen.

Words of Assurance

Hear the Good News. God's ways are not our ways. Ours is a God of mercy and forgiveness. All who will turn to God will be received joyously, pardoned abundantly, and will live forever in the love of God.

Benediction

May we who have known the forgiveness and grace of God go forth into the world to share that forgiveness and grace with all that we meet, friend and stranger alike. Peace be with us all, now and forever. Amen.

Fourth Sunday in Lent

Agnes W. Norfleet

Joshua 5:9-12: The Israelites celebrate the Passover in their new land and the manna ceases.

Psalm 32: Those whose transgression is forgiven are called happy; they are encouraged to pray to God, to let themselves be taught the way they should go, and to rejoice and shout for joy.

II Corinthians 5:16-21: In Christ we become brand-new creations, reconciled to God; we therefore are Christ's ambassadors, proclaimers of this message of reconciliation.

Luke 15:1-3, 11*b*-32: Jesus tells a parable about a prodigal son, an elder brother, and an unusual father.

REFLECTIONS

While I confess that I have resisted this argument, it has been brought to my attention by male friends and colleagues that, in general, men are getting pretty bad press these days, especially fathers. On television and in the movies men are more often than not portrayed in a negative way—coming across as one-dimensional characters, either heroically macho and violent, or babbling buffoons, or success driven and without emotion.

From *The Prince of Tides* to *Legends of the Fall,* in relationships, husbands and fathers frequently are portrayed as emotionally distant and inaccessible, the possible exception being a man named Forrest Gump, who suffers his own mental and emotional challenges. Occasionally this phenomenon of the negative portrayal of men gets pointed out to me at home. Not long ago our son James was sick, and I was enjoying one of those now rare moments when he was content to sit in my lap for an extended period of time just to be held. James and I were watching a videotape of the Beatrix Potter stories, based on her original illustrations. We had just finished *The Tale of Tom Kitten and Jemima Puddle-Duck* and were settling into *The Tale of Peter Rabbit and Benjamin Bunny.* Mopsy, Flopsy, and Cottontail were off to their good little bunny activity of picking berries. Peter Rabbit was putting on his little blue coat, and his mother was warning him to stay out of Mr. McGreggor's garden. She warns: "Remember your Father . . . was put in a pie by Mrs. McGreggor." With that, Larry, my husband, walked into the room, turned, and said, "That's just one more example of a father getting a bad rap."

Today's Gospel news is about an unbelievably good father.

A Sermon Brief

Jesus told parables so that, as with any good story, they could weave their way into the fabric of our lives in different ways. Stories invite us to hear and to draw our own conclusions. The risk we run with Jesus' parables is to become so familiar with them that we think we know exactly what they mean.

In order to recapture some of the gospel truth of this most familiar story, I want to share with you some recent biblical scholarship that has certainly shed light on this story for me. Kenneth Bailey has for forty years lived in the Middle East and studied the peasant culture in the part of the world where these parables of Jesus were first told. Just as the literature of the American South assumes a certain regional culture and set of values, Bailey holds that so do these Gospel parables. They are better understood in light of Middle Eastern culture. By situating this story in its cultural context, my hope is to reframe this familiar parable so that perhaps we can again be startled by the offensiveness of its grace.

A certain man had two sons. One day the younger son, having grown restless, asked his father if he might collect his inheritance early. So the father divided his property between them. About this opening detail, the setting of the stage, Bailey writes, "For over fifteen years I have been asking people of all walks of life from Morocco to India and from Turkey to the Sudan about the implications of a son's request for his inheritance while the father is still living. The answer has always been emphatically the same." The following conversation usually ensues:

"Has anyone ever made such a request in your village?"
"Never!"
"Could anyone ever make such a request?"
"Impossible!"
"If anyone ever did, what would happen?"
"His father would beat him, of course!"
"Why?"
"This request means—he wants his father to die!"[1]

"There is no law or custom among the Jews or Arabs which entitles the son to a share of the father's wealth while the father is still alive." The request made of a son to a father for his share of inheritance is the same as saying, "Father, I cannot wait for you to die."[2]

"In all of Middle Eastern literature (aside from this parable) from ancient times to the present, there is no case of any son, older or younger, asking for his inheritance from a father who is still in good health."[3] The story shatters cultural assumptions from the very beginning. "The father is expected to explode and discipline the boy for the cruel implications of his demand."[4] Even before the younger son runs off and squanders his money, to Jesus' hearers the request itself would have been unthinkable.

Soon after the younger brother got his share, he headed off to a far country. There he was caught up in wild, self-destructive living, so that before long he had lost all his money. He was reduced to feeding the pigs of Gentiles in order to stay alive. What good Jewish boy would get anywhere near pigs?

According to custom, family property lost to Gentiles was a serious matter, and a violation of the whole community. When the prodigal comes home, the village community would soon discover this. The townspeople may well do what the father did not do—punish the boy severely. Somehow, in his poverty and hunger, the son did come to himself and return home. With a face-saving plan he proposes to come home as a hired servant, the lowest of the servant classes, yet still a free man. As a hired servant he will be free to live independently in the village with his own income and perhaps to pay back what he lost, thus fulfilling his moral responsibilities to his father. He has offended the community, but he must go home because he is starving. The village mockery will simply have to be faced. He has a plan to meet the moral obligation owed to his father. In short, the prodigal comes home to save himself. He wants no grace.

"The Oriental farmer . . . lives in his village, not in isolation out on his land."[5] We can confidently assume that this father lives in a village as part of the community. The father also knows how the village will treat the boy upon his return—with slander and the thing feared most, the gathering of a mob. No doubt, he will be subjected to verbal and physical abuse. The father is fully aware of how his son will be treated, if and when he returns to the community he has rejected.

As the story goes, the child did return and when he was still a long way off, his father saw him and ran to welcome him. What the father does in this homecoming scene can best be understood as a series of dramatic actions calculated to protect the boy from the hostility of the village and to restore him to fellowship within the community. These actions begin with the father running down the road.

"An Oriental nobleman with flowing robes never runs anywhere. To do so is humiliating." Jewish tradition says: "A man's manner of walking tells you what he is."[6] It is very undignified in Eastern eyes for an elderly man to run. Aristotle claims, "Great men never run in public."[7] But the Bible says, "He had compassion," which specifically includes the awareness of the gauntlet the child will have to face as he makes his way through the village. "The father then runs this gauntlet for him,"[8] assuming a posture so humiliating in that culture that one would find it hard to believe. Reconciliation is made public at the edge of the village with the father's kiss, and therefore the "son enters the village under the protective care of the father's acceptance."

"Rather than experiencing the ruthless hostility he deserves and anticipates, the son witnesses an unexpected, visible demonstration of love in humiliation. . . . There are no words of acceptance and welcome." The father's running and kiss are acts that replace speech. "The love expressed is too profound for words."[9] We see in the father's actions that the point is not the lost money, or even the unforgivably bad behavior, but rather the broken relationship which the son cannot heal. The new relationship must be a pure gift from his father. Bring out a robe, the best one, which is certainly the father's robe. Put shoes on his feet! He's a free man. Kill the fatted calf! The whole village will be present that evening to accept and celebrate the return of this undeserving son. Before everyone in town, this son's repentance is the acceptance of the grace that is offered to him.

This father's love is like the love of God. The father takes on himself the humiliation due the child. The father becomes a self-emptying, suffering servant. The father runs the gauntlet for the child in a public, visible demonstration of love, a love which reaches the level of *cost* that becomes life-changing in its power.

When Jesus tells this story, Jesus is offering an image of himself as he makes his way to Jerusalem. Jesus will face what the prodigal deserves. Jesus will be met on the edge of town by a mob. Jesus will be mocked and beaten. Herod will put an elegant robe on him and send him back to Pilate. Jesus will be ultimately humiliated by death on a cross, but he will die saying, "Father, forgive them for they know not what they do." What wondrous love is this?

SUGGESTIONS FOR WORSHIP

Call to Worship (Ps. 32:11)

LEADER: Be glad in the LORD and rejoice, O righteous,

PEOPLE: **And shout for joy, all you upright in heart.**

Prayer of Confession

O God, we have been like a horse or a mule, without understanding. We have not allowed our temper to be curbed with bit and bridle. We have not stayed near you. And we have kept silence, forgetting to acknowledge our sin, hiding our iniquity, refusing to confess our transgressions to you. Forgive us, instruct us, and surround us with steadfast love, that we may declare, "Happy are those whose transgression is forgiven, whose sin is covered." Amen.

Assurance of Pardon (II Cor. 5:17 adapted)

Anyone who is in Christ is a new creation: everything old has passed away; everything has become new!

Benediction (Luke 15:24*b*; II Cor. 5:19; Ps. 32:7 adapted)

We who were dead are alive in Jesus Christ; we who were lost are found! Let us join Christ in the work of reconciling the world to God. And may God be a hiding place for us in times of trouble and surround us with glad cries of deliverance and homecoming and new creation.

---

1. Kenneth E. Bailey, *Poet and Peasant* and *Through Peasant Eyes: A Literary-Cultural Approach to the Parables of Luke* (Grand Rapids, Mich.: Eerdmans, 1983), p. 161.
2. Bailey, p. 162, citing L. Levison, *The Parables: Their Background and Local Setting* (Edinburgh: T. & T. Clark, 1926), p. 156.
3. Bailey, p. 164.
4. Ibid., p. 165.
5. Ibid., p. 180.
6. Ibid., p. 181.
7. Ibid., citing L. D. Weatherhead, *In Quest of a Kingdom* (London: Hodder & Stoughton, 1943), p. 90.
8. Bailey, pp. 181-82.
9. Ibid., p. 182.

Fifth Sunday in Lent

Patricia A. Spearman

Isaiah 43:16-21: God is about to bring the promise of restoration to fruition for Israel. As God gives us a new day each twenty-four hours, God promises to give new life to the chosen people. The failures of the past will be obliterated as God performs the miracle of restoration.

Psalm 126: The psalmist speaks of the euphoric feeling that accompanies restoration. Tears are replaced by laughter. Sorrow is giving way to joy. Seeds were sown in the midst of despair, but this great God of love has given her people a bumper crop in the harvest.

Philippians 3:4b-14: Paul claims the outward signs of purification do not fully address the forgiveness and healing of the soul. He is probably the best example in the New Testament of how God erases our past. When the cleansing power of the Holy Spirit washes our soul, we must accept the challenge of moving toward our ultimate potential, through Jesus Christ. Our past mistakes can enslave us, if we let them. Forgetting those things which are behind us liberates us to soar toward the prize.

John 12:1-8: This story could be titled, "Giving you the best that I've got." As a gift, Mary's anointing of Jesus pales in comparison to the gift of restoration and hope she has received from him through his ministry.

REFLECTIONS

Today we find ourselves in the untenable position of defending the rights of convicts to "start over." Crime has become so rampant in our societies, that people around the world demand that criminals be locked up, without hope of reentering the civilized world. I'm not suggesting that we do away with their personal responsibility to accept the consequence of their actions. I do, however, believe that we can learn a valuable lesson from the story recorded in John's Gospel. There are three basic elements that build to the climax of restoration:

1. Jesus is in the midst of people who seem to have it all together;
2. A woman with a spotted past comes to give a personal gift to the Lord; and
3. Those on the periphery who feel that her actions are a waste of time and of a valuable resource are condemned.

Although people find it difficult to forgive and accept the possibility of new life after penitence, Jesus is always available for the reconciliation that occurs in redemption. Mary is not identified as rich or as one with any particular clout. By all accounts she was just an ordinary person, who wanted to give an extraordinary gift. The oil represents the very best that she could do. She wanted to give her best to Jesus, who had given so much to her. It was more than appreciation for the resurrection of Lazarus; it was truly an appreciation for the hope she had through his affirmation of her personhood.

To those in the community she may have been a nobody, but Jesus treated her like a dignitary. Unlike Zacchaeus, she couldn't use her position in government to rectify the shortfalls of her past. All she had was the oil she'd saved for a rainy day. The story is punctuated by her boldness in approaching Jesus in spite of her gender or the crowd. Someone who has experienced the pain of midnight can appreciate the dawn of a new day.

A SERMON BRIEF

It's almost time for the big event. Everyone has come to town for the celebration. Caught up in the moment, they are unaware of the presentation that is about to take place. Jesus is sitting comfortably with friends and other admirers. Perhaps they were reflecting on the unprecedented miracle of Lazarus' resurrection. Maybe they were just chewing the fat about other miracles or the growing consternation of church officials.

Without warning, Mary walks in and begins to pour oil on the feet of Jesus. "What are you doing?" someone says. Undaunted by the accusatory question, she proceeds to wipe his feet with her hair. The fragrance fills the room and the entire house. Judas, the spokesman for those who wouldn't speak up, reproves Mary for wasting this precious resource. The unmitigated gall of this person.

No, she was not really a person in the eyes of society. She was just a woman—a creature just below other animals or items considered as chattel. Imagine a woman coming into the midst of the guys and interrupting their conversation with this irresponsible, wasteful act. Some may have discounted her (apparent) ignorance by blaming it on her gender. Everyone believed that women did not have the intellectual prowess of men. There was no way she could possibly have known the value of the oil or the price it could retrieve in the market. The intimation that the oil could be used to help with outreach may have been intended to cover the disdain of her accuser.

However, Jesus and Mary are caught up in the moment of reconciliation. Mary does not apologize for her actions, or make an attempt to explain them. Jesus comes to her defense. He speaks to her intent, not content. Jesus was in a position to know the hearts and minds of everyone in the room. They had gathered to prepare for the celebration of the Passover, the ritual kept by every good Jew. In the pre-celebration spirit, they were unaware of the real nature of their trip to Jerusalem. Jesus was on his way to pay the price for our salvation . . . with his life.

The writer leads us to believe that Mary was unaware of the symbolic light when Jesus defends her actions. For Mary, it was an opportunity to give something back to the Lord for all that he had given to her. It was a chance to let him know just how much he meant to her. There is no indication that her actions were premeditated and intended to upset the status quo. She simply saw an opportunity to give and seized the moment.

Much has been written about heroes, past and present. Although the scenarios differ, they all seem to say the same thing when asked why they responded in such a courageous manner. "I knew I had to do something, so I did it." I remember reading an account of Rosa Parks after the successful bus boycott to end segregated transportation in Montgomery, Alabama. In her unassuming manner, she said, "I was not trying to break the law. I was just tired." Mary did not give her gift as an act of protest. She simply wanted Jesus to know the depth of her appreciation.

As we approach the celebratory time of Easter, it's important to remember the woman who represents gratitude for restoration. New clothes, shoes, and hairstyles will not cover the real pain of our brokenness. If, however, we accept the redemptive love of Jesus, we can become new creations with a fresh start. Jesus comes to offer forgiveness for those things in our past that have kept us from a right relationship. Payment on the promise of restoration is within our grasp.

Like Mary, we have to be willing to seize the opportunity for wholeness. The journey of reconciliation starts in our hearts. It's not the content of the gift, but the content of our hearts that makes a difference. Let us decide today to bring our best gift to the Lord. In the madness of the moment, Jesus will take what we have and give us something beautiful in return.

Mary was more than just a woman. Formerly disgraced, she showed how grace is animated through Jesus. Through someone who was dismissed on the basis of her gender, Jesus showed how genetic calculations really don't matter. There will always be opportunities for mission work. It is important to remember the poor, distressed, and downtrodden. It is equally important to remember that salvation is not just a corporate experience. Jesus makes it a personal experience. Mary's gift to Jesus transcended time and tradition to bring us a story of hope and wholeness. In the name of the God who loves us, cares for us, and reclaims us. Amen.

Suggestions for Worship

Call to Worship

LEADER: Good morning, people of God. This is a time of celebration.

PEOPLE: **How can we celebrate in the midst of trials?**

LEADER: God keeps us in the midst of the trials. The strong arm of the Lord sustains us during our weakness.

PEOPLE: **What about our tears?**
Is there anyone who sees me when I cry?

LEADER: Rest assured, God sees every tear that you shed. God knows every pain that you feel. Weeping may spend the night, but joy is on the way.

PEOPLE: **We have sown in sorrow, is it possible to reap in joy?**

LEADER: Yes! God has promised good to us. This is a day the Lord has made. This is a day of personal opportunity. This is a day to bring all of who we are to the Lord. I invite you, once again, people of God to the celebration.

ALL: The Lord has done great things for us. We are indeed glad! We are ready to receive the richness of restoration. Let the celebrattion begin!

Prayer of Confession

Lord, we come now to your table. We have not done all that you've told us to do. Some things you've asked of us, we've left undone. We come without piety or a false sense of religion. We come to you now with all of our talent and faults. We present now our bodies as our sacrificial gift. Forgive us, wash us, and restore now the hope of salvation. It's not much, but please accept our offering. Help us to forget those things that are behind us and move toward the divine prize you have promised. Amen.

Assurance of Pardon

God knows who we are, where we've been, and what we've done. In spite of our humanness, God is determined to love us. In the name of the God who reclaims and restores, you are forgiven.

Sending Forth

We have come into this house, bringing our tears, faults, and sorrows. We praise you, God, for the opportunity to find joy in the midst of the madness. We go forth into the world to show and share the love we have experienced today. We will give you the best that we have!

Passion/Palm Sunday

Catherine Gunsalus González

Isaiah 50:4-9*a***:** God opens the prophet's ear, so that, taught by God the Vindicator and Helper, the prophet sustains the weary and withstands insults and injuries.

Psalm 118:1-2, 19-29: A familiar passage about cornerstones, the day that the Lord has made, the one who comes in the name of the Lord, and the steadfast love of God that endures forever.

Philippians 2:5-11: The early Christian hymn about Christ Jesus who is emptied, obedient, exalted, and praised.

Luke 19:28-40: The story of Jesus' entry into Jerusalem.

REFLECTIONS

The events of Palm Sunday are familiar to us. New meaning arises when we look beyond the lectionary passage and interpret the all-too-familiar events in the light of Luke 19:41-48. (Read vv. 41-42 and 44*b*, which appear only in Luke's account.)

Peace! How we seek for it! Whether it is peace between nations, between family members, or even within ourselves, we look for peace. The people of Jerusalem also sought peace, and yet Jesus says that the real things that would bring them peace have been hidden from their eyes. And the reason they cannot find true peace is because they "did not recognize the time of [their] visitation." Instead of peace, destruction is going to come. Of whom is Jesus speaking? Who did not recognize the visitation? There are two possibilities. He may be thinking of those officials who had not come out to greet him. After all, the group that waved palm branches were not the leading citizens of Jerusalem. Rather, they were "the whole multitude of the disciples," and they were generally fairly marginal to the whole society.

Or Jesus may be speaking both to those who had failed to acknowledge him and to the crowds that had greeted him. This seems at first to be unlikely, for surely those who had welcomed him as he rode to the city on the borrowed colt could not be accused of not recognizing the time of their visitation. They had recognized him enough to come and greet him, and even enough so that the officials could not attack him. (Read vv. 47-48.)

Who did not recognize the time of their visitation? It matters immensely whom we include here, for we speak not only of ancient peoples but also of ourselves. It would be much easier for us if we could assume that Jesus here speaks only of those who do not acknowledge him. They are the ones who cannot see the things that would give them peace. But if we include the whole multitude in this group, that comes much closer to us.

Look again at the multitude. On Palm Sunday they seemed to recognize him. Even during the week, their presence protected him. But we know that their mood changed by Friday. Once Jesus was in the hands of the rulers, once he no longer seemed to have power, then the recognition faded that in this man God was visiting his people. The multitude were generally the powerless. They looked to Jesus at first because it seemed that he could change things. For the same reason, the powerful of Jerusalem feared Jesus. But by Friday, all of that was changed. The powerful were back in charge, and the loyalty of the people switched back quickly. The words of Jesus apply to the multitude who greeted him as well as to those who did not. Friday showed that almost none of them really knew the time of visitation. Almost none knew the things that really make for peace.

The spiritual "Sweet Little Jesus Boy" puts this confession in words for all of us:

> Just seems like we can't do right,
> Look how we treated you.
> But please sir forgive us Lord,
> We didn't know 'twas you.

A SERMON BRIEF

On Palm Sunday, Jesus begins his visitation of Jerusalem—God coming incognito into the midst of his people. God "visits" his people the way health inspectors visit restaurants—without warning and concealed as an ordinary member of the community.

During Holy Week, the visitation of Jerusalem did not go well, in spite of the joy apparent on Palm Sunday. In fact, by Friday the people were at their worst. What can be expected for the future, except a terrible future when judgment is rendered? Jesus even gives a glimpse of such a future. There will be no peace because the people have not recognized the time of their visitation.

The disciples should have understood more than they did. The idea of a "hidden visitation" should have been clearer to them. Even as the long trek to Jerusalem had begun, Jesus had sent the disciples ahead of him, two by two, to proclaim that the kingdom of God was near, even in their preaching. (Read Luke 10:1-12.) In the work and words of these disciples the kingdom of God draws near a town. It is a moment of opportunity and choice. And then, when the disciples leave, the time of choice has gone; the visitation is over. If the kingdom has been recognized, then peace is given. If the kingdom is not recognized, then no peace but rather destruction is the character of the future.

The presence of God's kingdom or of God in our midst is not always the same. That is precisely what "visitation" implies. Rather, God's presence is like an unscheduled train pulling into a station. Those who are ready and see it can get on. Those who do not cannot catch it once it leaves.

On the basis of these two passages, three things need to be said:

One, peace has a peculiarly corporate character. The city of Jerusalem and the cities the disciples visit, as units, respond or fail to respond. The peace or the destruction comes to the whole city or to none of it. We can understand this, for peace involves living without fear of attack, and part of our own search for peace deals with nations or with groups in conflict in a community. We often "spiritualize" peace too much and forget that it indeed has corporate characteristics.

Two, God comes to visit us incognito. This is not something God did with Israel only; it happens with us today. From Luke 10 we can understand that the proclamation of the gospel is one of the ways this occurs. We cannot despise this however humble it seems. When the Word of God is preached, it is indeed God's word to us, though it comes clothed in human words.

It is not only in preaching that our visitation occurs. Remember the strong words of Jesus that come to us in the twenty-fifth chapter of Matthew's Gospel. (Read Matthew 25:34-40). The blessed have responded well in the time of their visitation, and they will have peace. The cursed have been found wanting, and there will be no peace for them.

God continues the incognito visitations. He meets us when we do not expect him—not only in our worship and our religious life when we are ready for him. God meets us in our corporate life, in the poor, in those with whom we deal in our daily, nonreligious lives.

Finally, God comes to visit us in weakness, not only in power. We like a God who seems ready to do something for us. On Palm Sunday when Jesus seemed powerful, the multitude followed. But when Jesus is Pilate's prisoner, the same multitude turned away from him and back to the old leaders who again seemed in control.

It is probably the same tendency in ourselves that causes us to fail to recognize Jesus in the homeless and the prisoner. What can they do for us? They have no power. We are more like that multitude on Palm Sunday than we like to think. The words of Jesus apply to us as well. We do not always know the things that make for peace; we do not know the time of our visitation. What can the future hold for us, other than the destruction held out for Jerusalem and those other cities?

Thankfully, Palm Sunday is not the last word of the gospel, nor is Good Friday. We may try to pass by this God who visits us incognito, but he will not let us be rid of him. Easter is that message—and it brings us both joy and fear, both judgment and redemption. The visitations continue, and with them, the renewed possibility that we might finally recognize the things that lead to peace, and choose them. That is the possibility this Holy Week brings to us.

SUGGESTIONS FOR WORSHIP

Call to Worship (Ps. 118:1-2, 26-28 adapted)

LEADER: O give thanks to the Lord who is good,

PEOPLE: **Whose steadfast love endures forever!**

LEADER: Let the people of God say:

PEOPLE: **God's steadfast love endures forever!**

LEADER: Blessed is the one who comes in the name of the Lord.

PEOPLE: **We bless you from the house of the Lord.**

LEADER: The Lord is God and has given us light.

PEOPLE: **Bind the festal procession with branches, up to the horns of the altar.**

LEADER: You are my God, and I will give thanks to you;

PEOPLE: **You are my God, I will extol you.**

LEADER: O give thanks to the Lord, who is good,

PEOPLE: **Whose steadfast love endures forever.**

Prayer of Confession

O Lord, we have ignored your presence in our midst. The times of our visitation have not gone well. We know that as communities and as individuals we have so often forfeited the peace that could have been ours. Forgive us for all of this failure. Grant that you will not cease to visit us and that we may, through your grace, choose the right way and recognize you in our midst. All of this we ask in Christ's name. Amen.

Sending Forth (Luke 19:38; 24:36*b*)

Blessed is the king who comes in the name of the Lord! Peace in heaven, and glory in the highest heaven! Peace be with you.

Maundy Thursday

Susan Karen Hedahl

Exodus 12:1-4 (5-10), 11-14: This passage reflects a rich history, told through the priestly tradition, of a spring festival reworked historically to commemorate the "passing over" of the Lord for the deliverance of Israel from the Egyptians. Of special significance and homiletical use is the focus on the meal of deliverance.

Psalm 116:1-2, 12-19: The psalm begins with a thanksgiving for healing and then in the latter verses moves to the issue of fulfilling vows. Faithfulness of God's beloved, even to death, shows the intensity of the relationship between God and God's people.

I Corinthians 11:23-26: This passage marks several historical strands of the tradition of the Eucharist: it refers to the "new covenant" mentioned in Jeremiah 31:31 and links the blood of Jesus to the fact that the Mosaic covenant was also ratified in blood. Homiletically, there is much to consider in the matter of handing on the tradition of a certain way of eating and drinking and the links with the Old Testament's tradition of sacred meals.

John 13:1-17, 31*b*-35: Did the fact that a woman anointed Jesus' feet prior to his last Jerusalem visit prompt Jesus to do the same later? Is this passage the marking of the first sacrament? The delicate play of those who serve and those served is significant, and at the nexus of these two is the issue of love.

REFLECTIONS

Maundy Thursday marks the beginning of the church's most intense reflection on the beginning of the triduum, that span of hours leading to the resurrection of Jesus, announced in the Easter vigil. While the act of sharing the bread and wine may be part of this service, its highlight is found in the Gospel text, the emphasis on Jesus' command to love as we have been loved by God. The worship may or may not contain the washing of feet as an example of this.

The preacher has many places on which to focus. Maundy Thursday is a service that is remarkable for its scriptural and spiritual contrasts; the light and the darkness; allegiance and betrayal; the actions of love and the deeds of darkness; the relationship between master and servant; the shattering of community and, most of all, the listeners' knowledge of the inevitability of events to come.

The texts for Maundy Thursday focus on community, both its continuity and its disruptions and violations. The texts also force the reader to ask, At this central point of the Christian faith story, where are the women? What roles did they play in all of this? The texts make us ask in this regard, what if . . . ?

Because the use and, therefore, the preparation of food figures in all the day's texts, one may creatively explore those who baked the bread, readied the wine, and prepared the eating places.

One may ask about the act of foot washing and its relationship to the earlier Holy Week text of the woman's anointing Jesus' feet (an incident mentioned in all four Gospels). What of Pilate's wife, who would dream on that Thursday evening of Jesus and his doom?

Did the breakup of Jesus' group of disciples mean that home life would return "as usual" for the women in the lives of the disciples? How were the women, that other part of the creation which Jesus' life and death would redeem, affected?

This beginning of the Passion story raises the proclaimer's awareness of women as participants and recipients of God's gracious actions in Jesus.

A SERMON BRIEF

Two years ago I received an anguished phone call from friends. Would I officiate at the funeral of their beautiful and only-twenty-one-year-old daughter? She had been my riding instructor and had been killed in a car accident. Her father, a commercial pilot, told me later that he often reflected on the sequence of events leading up to his daughter's death. Each time he had renewed his pilot's license, he was reminded of the importance of knowing what sequence of events could lead to an accident, and knowing when to stop certain events. Such knowing could mean life or death. What if . . . ? was the operative phrase here.

What if the young woman had finished her ride earlier? What if her appointment had been an hour later? What if the county had decided not to gravel the road that day? What if the pickup that hit her had not appeared so unexpectedly at the rise of the hilltop?

During this Holy Week, this week of the Passion, each day has given us texts to mark the path toward the Cross. There is an inevitability about the story toward Golgotha that grips us in a spiritual vise. What if things had been different?

The What if? question catches us all the time. What if Karen had been the recipient of the new cancer research? Would she be alive today? What if Bill had chosen not to take drugs? Would he have any kind of life now? What if you had married that person instead of the one you are now married to? What if our congregation had called a different pastor than the one we now have. What if . . . ? It is the question we ask out of both relief and pain.

Think with me of those mentioned in the Holy Week texts. In Monday's texts, the woman anoints Jesus' feet. Jesus tells Judas, Leave her alone because she is preparing me for burial. With this first verbal signal, we ask, What if . . . ?

And then there is Judas. Could he have stopped that incident in the garden, which, of course, was the culmination of many other acts? What if he had had a change of heart before taking the money and spilling the beans about Jesus' location? What if he had never dreamed of betraying Jesus in the first place?

But this day, this Thursday, shows us all too clearly how futile are our What ifs. Things are coming unraveled. Too much has happened, and like Humpty-Dumpty no one will put all of this together soon, at least in human terms. The progress of the inevitable catches at our hearts.

But it is possible to ask another kind of What if? as we think of the action that stands at the center of this Maundy Thursday, the action of Jesus' washing the feet of his disciples.

The common task of a servant is now performed by the disciples' teacher and master! Everyone is squirming. Everyone is embarrassed. Get a servant in here to do this! What can he be thinking of? If only Jesus weren't doing this menial act. But the crown of this story appears later in the chapter: "I give you a new commandment, that you love one another. Just as I have loved you, you also should love one another."

It is this verse that bids us consider the What ifs and the If onlys that consume our lives.

The Passion story is truly an acknowledgment of how rapidly things can fall apart among us, leading to everything from disenchantment to destruction, even death. Sometimes the sequence of events is something we create or participate in, and sometimes we are passive observers or even victims.

But in the events of this evening, we see not a bid to worry further about the What ifs of life, but rather to seize upon the assurance of what we have heard and can do—love, in the name of Jesus. It is this commandment that pulls us through and even beyond the What ifs and the If onlys that seize upon us periodically.

There is a "catch"' in what Jesus commands. We are to do for others "as he has loved us." What does this mean?

For us, the life, the ministry, that marches to the cross is the kind of love that we are called to engage in, the kind of love that helps us meet the what ifs and the If onlys.

And when we do meet them, our responses are different than they might have otherwise been in view of Jesus' command.

What if I had or had not done that? Love comes with forgiveness.

What if this terrible tragedy had not happened? Love comes with the comfort and mystery of the Cross.

What if . . . ? To which Jesus said in the midst of it all the one thing needful for us to hear: "as I have loved you."

There are moments, days, maybe years, when the darkness of the What ifs may rule over us. But Jesus invites us to respond to the gift of love, alive in the face of impending death.

SUGGESTIONS FOR WORSHIP

Call to Worship

To this room, among Jesus' disciples, to this meal and the expressions of true servanthood, you are welcome! May Jesus meet you in the service given by your sisters and brothers, and may you also do those acts of love in the name of the one who redeems you.

Prayer of Confession

On this holy, tragic night, forgive us for our sins, our failures to do and not to do toward one another as we ought. We ask for your forgiveness, and for the gifts of fortitude, courage, and graciousness to enact your love in our community. In your meal and your actions, O Jesus, enable us to respond with thankfulness and love. Amen.

Benediction

No benediction is given on this night.
All await in silence—the Cross.

Good Friday

Susan Karen Hedahl

Isaiah 52:13–53:12: These verses are the fourth servant song of the book of Isaiah. The interpretations of the figure of the servant vary; here it can mean Israel, or read christologically, specifically the Messiah. Out of the utter desolation of his abandonment for righteousness' sake, the covenant community is redeemed.

Psalm 22: The Gospel of Mark records a fragment of this psalm as uttered by Jesus on the cross (Mark 15:34). The loss of hope, the approach of death, the mockery and cruelty of the community finally end in a note of triumph. Despite all of this, God does not forsake God's beloved ones.

Hebrews 10:16-25: The sufferings, death, and new life of Jesus bring three demands/joys to the Christian community. First, we are invited to enter God's presence in Christ through "the blood of Jesus"; second, we are to proclaim our faith, "the confession of our hope"; and finally, all of this is to manifest itself in loving deeds toward others.

John 18:1–19:42: The phrase "Passion of Our Lord," relates to the meaning of the Latin word *passionis,* or "sufferings." The scope of John's description can hardly be taken in—a relentless narrative of cruelty, betrayal, physical and spiritual attack, and finally death. However, John's Gospel stresses the victory of the Cross! Before this the worshiper can only respond with both grief and joyful thankfulness to the Beloved who endured all of this.

REFLECTIONS

Preaching within the Good Friday context is part of a process of the ancient triduum, the three liturgical events of Maundy Thursday, Good Friday, and the culminating Easter vigil. The Good Friday worship is characterized primarily by meditation leading to adoration. The Cross is the focal point.

Proclamation is not absent but muted, allowing the chosen texts to speak their particular story. Any of the preacher's words on any of the texts point the worshipers to the place of their death and new life—the cross of Jesus Christ.

The preacher is in a strange land homiletically. It is a time to make fewer words lead the listeners to the silences of the heart. Furthermore, the proclaimer stands delicately between the grief of the crucifixion and the celebration of this victorious death. Human speech may only suggest, infer, cry out, keep company with grief. It is also a time for the woman preacher, who in her very being, poses the question, "What manner of man is this who dies for the sake of love?"

And so, whether it is called sermon, meditation, or homily, the preacher does not explain or expound, but out of her own being reflects and invites congregational response to this man of sorrows and love.

Good Friday proclamation, like that of Easter, is perhaps the closest the speaker may come to combining prayer, praise, and proclamation in one form. Poetry, prayer, the arts, and words interspersed with silence reveal and praise most appropriately the form on the cross.

Several years ago when I attended a performance of *St. Matthew's Passion* in St. Paul, Minnesota, the memories of Bach's great work were permanently entrenched in my heart as the music was enhanced by close to twenty dancers. What was shown was not explained but left with me as a form of benediction. Behind a shimmering, translucent silk screen, draped from the floor to the ceiling of the stage, the dancers began a silent tableau, enabling the audience to realize they were viewing Jesus' shroud. Dancing freely with the shroud and to Bach's music, they concluded their dance in a silent heap of dancers, covered, buried, prostrate, wrapped in the shroud.

What then are we to say to all of this? We are to proclaim in a lean, tensive, passionate way, the death and victory of Jesus Christ. It is a story needing fewer words than usual, but all of the heart.

A SERMON BRIEF

Within the devastating set of events leading to the cross, John's Gospel shows well the remarkable human ability to "pass the buck." Jesus needs to be eliminated, but who will take explicit responsibility for that? So, where does the buck stop? Certainly not with the high priest, Pilate, or some of Jesus' own colleagues. Even those who have professed their love for him are saying to the courtyard maids, "I never heard of the guy!"

This forward impetus toward destruction halts abruptly in John's Passion story with a remarkable, quiet scene at the foot of the cross. The narrative's temporary cessation of wickedness and hate makes this scene truly the eye of the storm, punctuated only by the words of Jesus. The issue of "Where does the buck stop?" is turned on its head. The currency of denial and repudiation becomes the coinage of recognition, love, and responsibility. The question is changed as are the respondents and the purpose. Instead, from the mouth of Jesus the question becomes "How might we receive one another now?" How can this happen? What might stop the stampede of wickedness?

John describes the three women at the foot of the cross in 19:25-27: Jesus' mother, Mary; the wife of Clopas, also named Mary; and Mary Magdalene. It is perhaps remarkable that they are there at all given the motives of hate and anger which have nailed their beloved son, nephew, and friend to the cross.

Jesus addresses his mother first, asking her to claim the beloved disciple as her son and, in turn, asking that disciple to claim Mary as his mother. What currency is this? What event has happened with Jesus' words at this point? On the spot adoptions are not the general run of any day's events.

The listeners witness the beginnings of the beloved community in and through which all who claim Jesus as Lord and Savior will find their identities, their names, and the source of their lives. But what does this sound like? It sounds like those who are present at a birth!

Like the protective and wise midwives of ancient Israel, Shiprah and Puah, confronting the Egyptian king to save the Israelite children (Exod. 1:15-22), these women also witness the birth of a new way of being for themselves and for others. At the foot of the cross, they and we witness an astonishing midwifery of the spirit! A birthing of a new community and new loves and affiliations!

Margaret of Oingt, a fourteenth-century prioress in France, recognized that in Jesus' death on the cross was a birth.

> Ah, who has seen a woman give birth thus!
> And when the hour of birth came, they placed
> You on the bed of the Cross.
> And it is not astonishing
> Your veins ruptured
>   As you gave birth in one single day,
>   To the whole world!

John's Gospel notes that once Jesus had said this, he "knew that all was now finished" (v. 28). The birth of the community which he had lived and would now die for was done. Was a life completed? Yes. Was a life begun on the cross? Indeed! With all the blood, pain, groaning, and violence of giving birth, the exchange between Jesus and those near him marked almost unseen and unheard the stupendous event of new life and community.

It was the exclamation point on the cross which few knew of then, but now lives vitally and powerfully in many times and places.

Suggestions for Worship

Call to Worship (based on Psalm 22)

LEADER: My God, my God, why have you forsaken me?

PEOPLE: **Why are you so far from helping me, from the words of my groaning?**

LEADER: Yet it was you who took me from the womb;
you kept me safe on my mother's breast.

PEOPLE: **On you was I cast from my birth, and since my mother bore me you have been my God.**

LEADER: All the ends of the earth shall remember and turn to the Lord.

PEOPLE: **And all the families of the nations shall worship God.**

Prayer of Confession

Unto your holy Cross, O Jesus, we cry!
For the sins of humanity, for our faults you give your life.
In your innocent blood, let us find forgiveness,
In your agonies, let us find grace,
In your love unto death, let us find life beyond death!

Assurance of Pardon (based on Heb. 10:19-22)

Therefore, my friends, since we have confidence to enter the sanctuary by the blood of Jesus, let us approach with a true heart in full assurance of faith, with our hearts sprinkled clean from an evil conscience. In the name of the One who died for us, Jesus Christ. Amen.

Benediction

May the cross of Jesus Christ defend you, grace you, and enliven you to new living and being!

Easter Day

Teresa L. Fry Brown

Acts 10:34-43: Peter preaches to Cornelius and his household.

Isaiah 65:17-25: God promises to create a new heaven and a new earth where no one will die too soon, all will "enjoy the work of their hands," and wolf, lamb, lion, and ox will live together without harm.

Psalm 118:1-2, 14-24: Israel gives thanks for God's steadfast love. The psalmist praises the Lord, "my strength," "my might," and "my salvation." The psalmist praises God for life after the threat of death, for an answer to prayer, for "the day that the Lord has made."

I Corinthians 15:19-26: Paul describes first the risen Christ as the firstfruits of all who have died and then the end of all things when all things are subject to God.

John 20:1-18: One account of the women's visit to the tomb on Easter morning and Jesus' commissioning of Mary Magdalene.

Luke 24:1-12: Another account of the women's visit to the tomb and their carrying news of Jesus' resurrection to the others.

REFLECTIONS

Exegetical gleanings and wrestlings: Psalm 118, I Corinthians 15, and Isaiah 65 were used in the call to worship, Easter prayer, and benediction.

They all speak of the difficulty—on the part of both believers and nonbelievers—of accepting God's reality: peace, the Messiah, and his resurrection from the dead. The "peace" of Isaiah 65:25—human, animal, ecological—is especially difficult for me to address in the face of the contemporary reality of sustained violence, abuse, murder, and death from disease. If the Messiah turned the world upside down, why does my thirteen-year-old daughter ask the same question I asked thirty years ago, "Mom, why doesn't God stop the killing?" The persistence of blatant sin in the world makes preaching about resurrection and new life difficult.

After selecting John 20, Acts 10, and Luke 24 for the sermon brief, I initially focused on the reasons the women, present at both the crucifixion and resurrection, were not believed. Then I wondered why the church continues to set some persons up as judge and jury to decide who is worthy to bring the word to other disciples. As I read and reread the texts, the concept that God does not show favoritism became clearer. Each preacher has an obligation to preach a liberating message—that Christ lives in all and commands all to "go, tell" (Mark 16:7), in spite of those who do not believe the messenger and without apology for or argument about women's presence.

A SERMON BRIEF

What time is it? It's been dark for so long. Yesterday was just awful. The blood, the hammering, the dust, the agony, the laughter, the tears, the cries, the earthquake, the blood. He wouldn't come down to save himself. He stayed there for so long, but they said it was three hours. Dismas and Gestas deserved to die, but he didn't. What time is it?

He loved us so. Forgave me for what I had done. He loved us so. Even when we slept outside or had little to eat, no comforts of home, he loved us. Even when we forgot who he was, he still loved us. He said he was going away, but we need him here. What time is it?

No tomb, we had to use Joseph's. Had to beg the soldiers to let him be taken away so no one would touch his body. We need to get there as soon as possible to wash him and place the oils on his body for burial. He said something about coming back in three days, but I didn't understand him. What time is it? Isn't it morning yet? Got to go; got to go and see my Lord one more time.

The scriptures report that early in the morning on the first day of the week the women—Mary Magdalene, Salome, Mary, the mother of James, Joanna, and others—went to the place where Joseph of Arimathea had laid Jesus' body. They went to prepare him for final entombment. As they arrived, they noticed that the soldiers were gone and the gravestone was rolled away. Angels appeared, asking them why they were seeking the living among the dead. Jesus is not here. Look for yourself. The grave clothes are neatly folded. He is gone.

Can you imagine what went through Mary Magdalene's mind? The one she loved so dearly was gone. Was it grave robbers? No, things were not disturbed. Did he really rise from the dead? Have you ever waited and waited for something to happen and when it did you could not believe it? You know, like when you wait for the baby to be born and she finally arrives! What a miracle! You have worked and worked for ordination or a promotion. You have been turned down, turned back, deferred, repeatedly. Now they are telling you you passed. It's your harvest time. You have tenure. Your salary has been increased. What do you do? Do you think they are lying? Maybe you should go to the bishop or your dean or the boss in person and check out the details. Then you may believe it. When you can see, hear, touch, taste, and smell it, then you begin to believe.

The good news of Easter is that Christ rose as he said and that God, not humans, ordained which witnesses received the information and began the process of sharing it with the entire world. Mary Magdalene, like each of us, had to know for herself that Jesus had risen. This is the key to our faith—personal knowledge of the risen Christ. Mary did not immediately recognize the Christ and, when she did, she fell to her knees, clinging to him. He had been the first man to recognize that she was fully human, equal to others. He was the one who led her to turn her life around. And now, risen from the dead, Jesus says he must go and she must carry the message to the disciples.

Some commentators say that the women were afraid; some say Mary Magdalene wept; others say she ran to tell the disciples that Jesus rose. Whatever she did, she was the one who carried the first message of Christ's resurrection, his rebirth. Just as Mary the mother of Jesus carried the Savior into the world, this Mary carried the word of newness in Christ within her spirit to the world. God does not show partiality. God uses whomever God wants to send the message of Christ into the world. God has no regard for nationality, possessions, class, gender, character, work, or station. God wants messengers who preach a good word of reconciliation and regeneration. Because of her willingness, Mary found joy in the morning, another opportunity to see her Lord.

In her January 20, 1993, inaugural poem, "On the Pulse of Morning," Maya Angelou issued an invitation:

> Lift up your faces, you have a piercing need
> For this bright morning dawning for you
> . . . .
> Give birth again
> To the dream.

(Maya Angelou, *On the Pulse of Morning* [New York: Random House, 1993])

Mary, the other women, and the disciples would learn what we must learn. When the pain subsides, when the morning breaks, when the darkness passes, joy will come. The joy of the Lord is our strength. Only John immediately saw and believed. The others did not immediately understand what had happened, but in time they would. They would soon undertake the mission that Jesus the Christ taught them: "There is plenty good room in God's kingdom." Soon they would go forth and live out the reason that Christ died and rose for all our sins. Christ came to give each of us life, to remove barriers, to obliterate social stigmas, to open up the way to heaven for all of God's children who "truly and earnestly repent of their sins and are in love and charity with their neighbors" (A.M.E. Communion ritual, *African Methodist Episcopal Church Hymnal* [Nashville: A.M.E. Church Press, 1984], 12). Even Peter, who ran to the tomb after hearing the news from Mary, had to learn to move past his rigid prejudices in order to preach to Cornelius, a Roman centurion. When the word of God took root in Peter's heart, he was able to move past his Jewish heritage and Cornelius's gentile background and do the work of God. Peter had to move to God's agenda, not to what was politically expedient.

The good news of the resurrection is that if we wait, God will be present in our lives. If we look past the tombs of oppression into the light of day, we will see possibilities for change. Mary had to wait until morning so she could feel the living presence of the Lord. Sometimes it takes a while to find the tunnel before we can seek the light at its end. The morning is a clean slate washed of the filth of the preceding day by God's refreshing dew.

So, my sisters and my brothers, wait for the joy in the morning. The scriptures teach us that "weeping may endure for a night, but joy cometh in the morning" (Ps. 30:5*b* KJV). Wait for the joy in the morning. How long, Lord? Not long. Wait for the joy in the morning. Rest assured that God will do just what God has promised. We serve a God who hears and answers our prayers with "Yes," "No," or "Wait." Wait, my sisters, for the dayspring when all things are made brand-new. Don't give up when they will not hear you. Preach the message of salvation. The morning is coming. Wait, my brothers, do not be discouraged when they say you lack proper gifts to serve God. Tell the word about Jesus and his love anytime, anyplace, and anywhere you can raise your voice. Wait for the joy that comes in the morning.

Let us imagine we are going to the entrance of the tomb each morning of our lives to remind ourselves that he is not there, he is risen from the dead, and he is Lord. Let us search our hearts to ensure that we are still serving an equal opportunity God who says there is room enough at the cross for each of us. Let us raise our voices to tell the world that "He lives, He lives, Christ Jesus lives today!" When people ask you how you know your Savior lives, say, "He lives within my heart" (Alfred H. Ackley, "I Serve a Risen Saviour," The Rodeheaver Co., 1933, renewed 1961).

SUGGESTIONS FOR WORSHIP

Call to Worship (based on Ps. 118:1, 22, 24)

LEADER: O give thanks unto the Lord who is good and worthy of all our praise.

PEOPLE: **Praise the Lord for renewed lives, renewed hopes, renewed dreams, and renewed spirits.**

LEADER: This is the day that the stone that the builders rejected rose from the grave with all power in his hands.

PEOPLE: **We commit ourselves to building up what the world has torn down and redeeming the souls of our families, churches, and communities.**

LEADER: Let us praise and worship the one who is our hope for today and tomorrow.

PEOPLE: **Let us never be ashamed to tell the world who delivered us from our distresses and cleansed us from our sins.**

ALL: **This is the day that all things are made brand-new, we will rejoice and be glad in it. Amen.**

Easter Prayer

God of power, promise, and possibility, we come rejoicing in your victory over death and the grave as we celebrate the knowledge that Christ lives today. Your promise that "old things will pass away and all things will become new" is evident in the forgiveness we experience as we petition you to cast into the sea of forgetfulness all our doubts, fears, and mistrust of you and one another. God of a second chance, you have opened our hearts and minds to new opportunities to live as Christ taught us. God of Adam and Eve, Isaac and Rebekah, Jacob and Rachel, Mary and Joseph, Paul and Mary Magdalene, you continue to provide new possibilities for living in love and peace with our sisters and brothers. Help us to continue to look for you in unexpected places and in the faces of one another. Amen.

Sending Forth

Rejuvenating Lord, our blessed Redeemer, be present with us as we travel into the world that we might each become shining stars, witnesses of the beauty of your empowering, sustaining, and healing love. Help us to help others see you, not in the cold, dark tombs of life, but in the beauty of the gardens of renewal. Amen.

Second Sunday of Easter

Christine M. Smith

Acts 5:27-32: Peter and other apostles defend themselves before the council.

Psalm 118:14-29: Easter themes here include: "glad songs of victory," "the right hand of the Lord does valiantly," "the stone that the builders rejected has become the chief cornerstone," "this is the day that the Lord has made," "God . . . has given us light. Bind the festal procession with branches, up to the horns of the altar."

Psalm 150: The people, in fact everything that breathes, are called upon to praise God using a variety of musical instruments.

Revelation 1:4-8: John begins his Revelation, including his vision of Jesus' "coming with the clouds."

John 20:19-31: Jesus appears to ten of the disciples on Easter evening; a week later he appears again and converses with Thomas.

REFLECTIONS

The two issues in this Johannine text that captured my passion and attention were: (1) acknowledging and confronting the power of human fear, and (2) "re-imagining and re-imaging" Thomas. The setting of the text confronts us with the disciples' fear. Persecution is a very real possibility. How will we as preachers speak about this fear without speaking words that are anti-Semitic? I chose to speak in a more general way about the kind of fears that keep many of us behind locked doors. Another sermonic approach might be to focus much more specifically on the distinctive realities of oppression and the impact persecution has on concrete human beings. Perhaps hiding and fear are reasonable responses to potential violence. Ultimately, the text confronts us with the truth that wherever we are, and whatever the reasons we remain behind locked doors and in hiding, the power and possibility of the resurrected Christ is able to find us.

Even though many scholars believe that John's portrayal of Thomas is not one of judgment, but rather paradigmatic of human doubt, this interpretation still seems inadequate. Thomas longs to come closer to the resurrected Christ. He wants to see the marks of the nails. He wants to put his fingers in those marks and his hand in the wounded side. Thomas needs presence in order to believe and to participate in resurrection life. His vulnerable, honest stance leads me to believe he is more paradigmatic of faithful searching than disbelieving doubt. Perhaps most of us need to experience resurrection concretely before we can wholeheartedly proclaim, "My Lord and my God!"

A SERMON BRIEF

"When it was evening on that day, the first day of the week, the doors of the house where the disciples had met were locked for fear. . . ." Fear is a powerful thing in our lives. It prompts us to seek protection in times of very real danger. It motivates us into needed changes and surprising adventures. It serves as a constant reminder that we are fragile, limited, human.

On the other side of these life-giving impulses, we know fear also prompts us to "lock the doors of our lives" from the mystery and wonder of the unknown and run into places of isolated hiding. Very few emotions are stronger than fear; very few experiences are as awesome and full as those moments in life when we feel genuinely afraid.

Mary Magdalene and some of the disciples have discovered an empty tomb, and the doors where the disciples are meeting are locked for fear. Mary has heard her own name spoken by her beloved teacher and friend, and the doors where they were meeting are locked for fear. I can't help wondering, as I ponder this resurrection story, whether Jesus' followers were afraid of death or afraid of life?

Resurrection life, which leaves tombs empty and grave clothes loosened and undone, is not always such a glorious and joyful thing. Resurrection life, which speaks our name and commissions us to speak its power to others, is rarely embraced by us with abandonment and celebration. Resurrection life, which holds out wounded hands and pierced bodies and invites us to see and touch, is seldom what we would boldly choose. I can't help wondering, are Jesus' followers afraid of death or terrified of life?

Leonardo Boff, a liberation theologian from Brazil, helps us understand why resurrection life is the wonderful and terrifying thing that it is: "Wherever, in mortal life, goodness triumphs over the instincts of hatred, wherever one heart opens to another, wherever a righteous attitude is built and room is created for God, there the Resurrection has begun" (*When Theology Listens to the Poor* [San Francisco: Harper & Row, 1988], p. 132).

I find these words incredibly beautiful and true, and I also know the work, the capacity, the courage, the pain out of which resurrection life emerges. Instincts of hatred are unbelievably difficult to overcome. It takes a lifetime to nurture a heart that truly has the capacity to be open and changed by another. Righteous attitudes and truths one can stake one's life upon are possible to find, but rare. And creating room for God often means relinquishment and single-mindedness.

Perhaps the real hope lies in the affirmation that when these things happen in mortal life, there resurrection has begun. Resurrection is a process, a turning, a striving, a stirring. Perhaps it has as much to do with how we are moving forward as where we end up. It has everything to do with being called forth from places of hiding and unlocking closed doors.

"When it was evening on that day . . . the doors of the house were locked for fear . . . Jesus came and stood among them and said, 'Peace be with you.' After he said this, he showed them his hands and his side."

I find it strange that so many interpretations of this particular resurrection story have named it a story about "doubting Thomas," and his need for tangible signs of Jesus' presence. Thomas simply asks to experience what Jesus has so freely given the others. Jesus does not condemn Thomas; he simply says, "Have you believed because you have seen me? Blessed are those who have not seen and yet have come to believe."

Let's be honest. Don't most of us need tangible, concrete experiences to bring us closer to resurrected life? The more I think about the courage that is required of us to face the claims and expectations of resurrection life, the more admiration I gain for Thomas. Unlike the other disciples who simply see, Thomas longs to come close, to embrace, and to touch. Thomas needs a presence that will transform, clarify, and compel. Thomas knows what he needs in order to enter into the power of resurrection life and asks for it. Sometimes we do not even know what we need in order to move into new life, but it comes as a painful gift and shocking surprise.

A few months ago I watched the movie *Separate But Equal*, a depiction of the historical time in U.S. history when the Supreme Court was debating the issue of desegregation in our nation's schools. For months the court is divided. While many of the justices believe that segregation is morally wrong, they humanly want to hide behind historical precedent and the risk of political and social turmoil. There are many turning points in the movie, but one is particularly memorable. Chief Justice Earl Warren takes a weekend trip to see Civil War landmarks with his African-American aid Mr. Patterson. That night we see Earl Warren eating a fine meal while reading Carl Sandburg's *Abraham Lincoln*. The next morning he comes out of the inn and sees Mr. Patterson sleeping in the backseat of the car. "Mr. Patterson, why are you sleeping in there?" Mr. Patterson replies: "I couldn't find a place. . . . Sir, there's no place within twenty miles of here where I . . ." The sentence doesn't need to be finished. Chief Justice Warren is never the same again. We next see him sitting with one of the other justices, saying: "The court must vote to desegregate. It is a moral issue, one that goes deep into the soul of our nation."

Resurrection has to do with being called forth from all kinds of hiding. Resurrection begins wherever one heart opens to another, wherever righteous attitudes are built, wherever goodness triumphs over the instincts of hatred. While nine White supreme court justices were debating an issue, Black men, women, and children were still sleeping in the backseats of cars. Concrete human encounters and experiences birth and sustain resurrection life.

Jesus understood our human need for presence. The same one who washed feet, broke bread, and ate with strangers, comes into the disciples midst, urging them to be at peace and commissioning them with the power of the Holy Spirit. Into their fear he comes, despite locked doors, disbelief, and hiding.

"When it was evening on that day, the first day of the week, the doors of the house where the disciples had met were locked for fear." I can't help but wonder, are Jesus' followers afraid of death, or terrified of life?

SUGGESTIONS FOR WORSHIP

Call to Worship

LEADER: We gather this Sunday after Easter longing to immerse our lives in the power of resurrection.

PEOPLE: **We desire to see and touch the Christ among us, and to have our Christian commissioning renewed.**

LEADER: We come to celebrate that the presence of resurrection finds us in the midst of our fears, and despite locked doors and hiding.

PEOPLE: We come to worship a God whose resurrection power knows no barriers, no ultimate constraints, and no limits. Amen!

Prayer of Confession

We are a people who know fear and hiding well. We find it painful to see and acknowledge the multitude of ways we live our lives behind locked doors. We want to be immersed in new beginnings, healing transformations, and resurrection moments, yet we see a world surrounded by suffering, pain, and death. We long for the power of Easter, yet we perpetually dwell in the season of Lent. We come this Eastertide season to have our resurrection courage renewed and stirred. We want to believe that even though we are complicit in so much human pain, suffering, and oppression, we can be commissioned once more to be an Easter people. Amen.

Assurance of Pardon

Within the embrace and encouragement of this religious community, we are always empowered to begin again. By the power of God's unspeakable mercy and unlimited resurrection power, we are sent again into the world bearing hope. Thanks be to God!

Sending Forth

Restore our courage, strengthen our hearts, and move our bodies out into your world once more. Release us from our fears, O God, sending us forth this day to be the bearers of resurrection hope.

Third Sunday of Easter

Christine M. Smith

Acts 9:1-6, (7-20): Saul is confronted by Jesus on the road to Damascus; in the longer passage, he is received into the church by Ananias, a disciple.

Psalm 30: A psalm of praise that God has "turned my mourning into dancing," "taken off my sackcloth and clothed me with joy."

Revelation 5:11-14: John hears first the thousands of thousands around the throne and then every creature in heaven and on earth singing praise to the Lamb.

John 21:1-19: Jesus appears to the disciples, who have returned to their fishing, and converses with Peter.

REFLECTIONS

Most scholars believe that John 21 is an appendix to the Gospel of John. Even though some verses sound like Johannine literature, most of the material stands in real contrast to the rest of the Gospel. The unknown authorship and the out-of-sequence character of these final verses do not diminish the chapter's challenge and its ability to speak to the ancient and contemporary Christian church.

Even though it is tempting to focus one's total attention on Peter, it would be unfortunate to miss the religious and vocational challenge offered to all gathered that day by the Sea of Tiberias. It is especially meaningful to see once again how the resurrected one comes into their midst, even though they may have temporarily abandoned their newfound work for the momentary work of fishing. In all the resurrection accounts in John, Jesus as the resurrected Christ comes without judgment or condemnation to help his followers renew their passionate commitments and their religious vocations.

This final chapter of John challenges us to be concrete and specific about tending and feeding. Even though preachers have often uprooted Jesus' words from the historical and social realities of the disciples' day, his words are never an abstract mandate. This mandate will surely take us where we do not wish to go, as surely as it will immerse our lives in resurrection hope and meaning. Perhaps the primary task behind this passage is for preachers to help individuals and whole communities of faith renew their commitments to tend and feed in an age of immense starvation and violence.

A SERMON BRIEF

In the face of tragedy and pain, sometimes it's good to return to that which is familiar. Some of the disciples are gathered by the Sea of Tiberias, and Peter decides to go fishing. Why would we expect anything else from one who was quick to declare his beliefs, and sometimes slow to understand them. He needs to think, to gather himself together. What better place than a fishing boat, what better time than the quiet, haunting calmness of the night. He needs this night, for what is about to happen in the morning will shock him, foretell his future, and challenge him to defend his ultimate loyalties.

I've often wondered what the beloved disciple (probably John), and then Peter, saw on the beach that morning that made them recognize "the Lord." But once Peter recognized the Lord, he leaped into the water, swimming toward the resurrected one with wild abandon. But resurrection presence and power are seldom what we expect, and almost always costly. What he found on that shore that morning was a familiar sacramental meal, and a stinging cross-examination. Peter is asked not once, but three times, if he will respond to the world as a faithful disciple. So typical of his passion, he responds with a resounding reaffirmation of his love. He promises he will do what Jesus mandates. Instead of praising his declarations, Jesus tells Peter that one day he will stretch out his hands and someone else will take him where he does not wish to go. This is not a happy message, a truthful one, yes, but far from comforting. He was told earlier that he would betray the Christ, now he is being told he will die a martyr's death. This is an offensive and terrifying picture of resurrection life. Feeding lambs and tending sheep can cost us our lives. It is not romantic or abstract. It is work that will link our lives to every form of pain and suffering we can imagine. It will lead us many places we do not wish to go.

When I want to be reminded of what feeding lambs and tending sheep really look like in our contemporary lives, I return to the movie *Romero*. The film focuses on a segment of the life and ministry of Archbishop Oscar Romero of El Salvador. He is a man who loves his people and the institutional church; he is struggling to know how to be faithful to them both. In the beginning, he works hard to keep the Christian church and the political repression of the country separate. It is as if a whole land of people are taking him where he does not want to go. In the end, he is assassinated because he has become one of the most outspoken voices of truth and confrontation. His is a journey toward both the mandate that confronts Peter in this text and toward resurrection.

One of the most haunting and inspiring scenes in the movie takes place after one of the churches within his realm of responsibility has been taken over by the military and no one is permitted to enter. The church has been turned into a barracks. Archbishop Romero walks past the guards at the entrance to the church, down the center aisle, and up to the altar. He tells the guard that they have come to remove the host, the body of the Eucharist. The guard laughs, turns, and with a machine gun opens fire across the entire altar area. Romero leaves and walks outside the church. He looks into the faces, the eyes, the silent courage of the people. Then he walks back inside the church, bends down on his hands and knees, and picks up pieces of the host in his hands. All the while, the same guard fires his gun over Romero's head. Romero walks out of the church and drives away in a car, only to return moments later. He steps out of the car, puts on his alb and his stole, and leads the people past the guards back into their church.

Feeding lambs and tending sheep ask of us that we put on whatever stole is ours to wear and that we walk bravely into the world with resurrection power and hope. It demands of us that we leap out of familiar boats into waters over our head and that we engage in sacramental meals on beaches and shorelines, in alleyways and hospital rooms, in desolate, lonely places where people are lost and afraid. Jesus is calling Peter and all the disciples to go there freely. Yet we know all too well that the compelling call of human need often feels like it is taking us to places we do not want to go. Our ability and willingness to go there will be a testimony to the clarity and passion of our Christian discipleship.

Anthony Padovano writes about the unrelenting power of resurrection life and urges us to embrace it with everything we are: "Life is what you must affirm no matter how painfully, even unwillingly. . . . [You are] reliable only when [others] ascertain they will always find life in [your] presence. Others must know you as faithful, faithful so often that when they wonder where life lives, they will think of you as one of those in whom life has made a home" (*Dawn Without Darkness* [Garden City, N.Y.: Image Books, 1982], p. 207).

Jesus is there on the beach that morning to ask each of the disciples one last time if they will make a home for life, a home that is so reliable, so persistent, so faithful, that everyone they touch will find life in their presence. He is asking them to resist the powers of death and suffering by making a home for life. And he does not mince words with Peter about the cost of such homes and the cost of such feeding.

This Eastertide let us renew our resolve to make a home for life. Let us feed and tend until every human being and all creation have experienced resurrection life. Let us prepare holy meals the world over, and let us pick up our vocation freely. Let each one of us individually, and all of us together, decide again to put on whatever stole enables us to be the people of God in the world.

SUGGESTIONS FOR WORSHIP

Call to Worship

LEADER: We come into community once again, O God, so that we might discover anew the meaning of our discipleship in your world.

PEOPLE: **We come to hear our names spoken and to be challenged to new life.**

LEADER: We come from all the places of our lives to praise you, O God, and to express thanks for the distinctive Christian call you give each one of us.

PEOPLE: **We come, O God, open and ready for your spirit and your leading. Amen.**

Prayer of Confession

Gracious God, we are a people who come from many places in life. We come from places of anxiety and pain. We come from places of confusion and despair. We come from places of guilt and shame. We come from places of need and longing. We come from places of joy and celebration. We are a people who lose sight of your claim and our call. We are not always able to see the resurrection life calling to us from the shore. We are not always able to love you and our neighbors as passionately and faithfully as we would like. We are not always able to move into places of suffering and injustice with healing and liberating power. Accept our human limitations, and rekindle our commitments this day. Amen.

Assurance of Pardon

In every moment of life, resurrection hope is held out to us again, and the possibility of transformation is available. With God's power to raise the dead up out of the grave, we, too, are raised from the dead places in our lives to vibrant life. Thanks be to God.

Sending Forth

Let us go into the world with stoles around our shoulders and bodies ready to swim toward resurrection life. In the face of a multitude of deaths, let us make strong and glorious homes for life.

Fourth Sunday of Easter

Teresa L. Fry Brown

Acts 9:36-43: Peter raises Tabitha from the dead.

Psalm 23: God is our Shepherd and our Host in the presence of our enemies.

Revelation 7:9-17: John sees the multitude that no one can count standing and worshiping before the throne of God and the Lamb.

John 10:22-30: Jesus promises to protect his sheep so that no one will snatch them out of his hand.

REFLECTIONS

Personal note: References to the resurrection are standard in every African-American sermon. Without them, a sermon is not a kerygmatic sermon. I particularly like to preach resurrection texts because of my personal experiences with oppression and overcoming restrictions in school, discrimination in business, and health problems.

Exegetical gleanings/musings: Revelation 7:12 and Psalm 23 were used to formulate the call to worship. John 10 is included in the prayer of confession. The image of Christ's holding the believer in his hand is a powerful image of ultimate protection. The universal possibility of resurrection and eternal life for men and women, Jew and Gentile, established believer and new Christian, as detailed in both John 10 and Acts 9, is captivating. Finally, the promise of "a new heaven and new earth" in Revelation 7 and the number "that no one could count," which is over and above the 144,000 representatives of Israel, underscore the inclusivity of the gospel and point to the inclusion of the dispossessed—any group usually voted out by power structures. These dispossessed will be included because God makes the final selection of those allowed into heaven.

The text on Tabitha could be useful in a study of women's roles, networks, or relationships in the context of both the biblical story and contemporary life. (Notice Tabitha's unselfish work with the widows. Why widows?) This is also a good text for a refreshing stewardship sermon. Here it will be used as a text about perseverance and faith. I tried to avoid two dangers: giving false hope of overcoming a catastrophic or terminal illness, and suggesting that loved ones may have died because they did not possess enough faith or were not good enough for God to consider saving.

A SERMON BRIEF

Why do we go to church? Why do we preach about or sing to or serve a God who at times seems so far away? As we strive to find a place to breathe freely in an often hostile world, where many of us are told we are nothing or nobody, why do we keep on trying to do right? How do beaten, abused, denied persons learn to love and worship God?

Come with me to ancient Tel Aviv, or Joppa, to the first resurrection story following Christ's resurrection. Our sister Tabitha (her Greek name is Dorcas) bears witness to the eternal power and protection of God for all souls who do the will and work of God regardless of what happens in their lives. Tabitha was a single, independent woman in a society where women were property, appendages of men, supported by fathers, brothers, or husbands. Tabitha is the only woman in the New Testament referred to as a disciple. Here we find Tabitha making clothing for widows and orphans, possibly holding religious meetings in her home. She apparently did not sell the clothes in order to profit from the misery of others, and she did not send the clothes anonymously—like those today who write a check to a charity organization for the faceless poor. She knew these widows and orphans. Perhaps she invited them into her home and shared her joy with them. The text does not tell us what happened in her life. It tells us instead that this woman of Christian charity died.

The custom in Palestine, because of the intense heat, was to wash the body, a purification ritual, and to bury it by sundown. Tabitha's body, however, was washed, wrapped, and laid in the upper room where the widows mourned for her, perhaps praying for the possibility that she would return to them.

Two brothers, who must have known what she meant in the community, traveled to Lydda to tell Peter that Tabitha had died and that he should come to Joppa as soon as possible. Why Peter? Hadn't he been present during three of Jesus' resurrection healings—Jairus's daughter, the widow's son, and Lazarus—and at the tomb following Jesus' own resurrection? Upon arriving, Peter met the widows gathered around Tabitha's body. Peter had a relationship with the Jesus who had healed the sick, raised the dead, fed the hungry, comforted the grieving, clothed the naked, and forgiven sins. Peter knelt but did not pray in his own strength. He prayed to the God of resurrections. When he heard from God, he got up, extended his hand, and told Tabitha to rise. She arose from the dead. He returned this sister of charity to the saints and widows who had prayed for her deliverance. They now rejoiced, and their faith was deepened.

But that was then. Where, you might ask, is our present hope that God is still in the business of saving, raising, and empowering God's children? Twenty years ago I was diagnosed with cervical cancer. After the shock, denial, anger, and acceptance of the doctor's options, I began to ask God, "Why?" Didn't I go to church my entire life, sing in the choir, work with the missionaries, teach Sunday school, try not to bother anybody, and just do what the Bible said do? Yet here I was twenty-five years old, being told I was going to die. I had so many things to do that Black people were just being allowed to do—become a lawyer, live where I wanted to live, travel—but now it seemed as if God would take me away at the beginning stages of my adult life. I was tired of fighting, tired of doing right. And what was the reward? Death. But I had a praying mother.

My mother was a church musician. She was at church it seemed all the time, and she was raising seven children. As she sat in my hospital room, humming softly, she prayed. I felt a little hope as I underwent surgery and placed my life in God's hands. I thought of the times when someone had spit in my face or called me a name or threatened to kill me if I didn't stay in my place, and I had the blessed assurance that the same God who kept me then was able to bring me out of the surgery. I was slow coming out of the anesthesia. The doctors said, "We thought we lost you. Your mother was here the whole time praying and said not to give up because God told her you would make it." I remember while I was under the anesthesia, I observed my funeral from the upper right-hand corner of a big screen, and people were rejoicing in my home-going. Then a voice said, "Not yet, Teresa, go back. There is much work for you to do."

That was twenty years ago and I still believe the words, "I don't feel no ways tired. . . . Nobody told me that the road would be easy, I don't believe [God] brought me this far to leave me." God included me in the plan of salvation, and I must continue to do God's appointed works to remain under full coverage by that plan. I feel washed and raised and empowered to go on in spite of what happens to my physical body. Yes, the world is still filled with destructive persons who seek to destroy and deny. Yes, there is at times confusion over who is in charge. But, we must continue to witness that God is still God and is able to "do exceedingly abundantly above all that we ask or think" (Eph. 3:20 KJV). My mother prayed, just as the widows prayed for Tabitha. My mother believed that God had a plan for my life.

In our humanness we get weak; sometimes fatigue stalls us in the midst of progress; we want to do good but evil surrounds us. God has promised to redeem us, to lift us up above that which seeks to destroy us. God gives us another opportunity each and every day to do the work we are sent to do. In spite of what others say or do, we are challenged to do all we can while we can, for tomorrow is not promised.

John the Revelator writes that there is a number that no one, not computer experts or projectors of population growth, can number, who will walk up the highway to heaven. These are they who come to great tribulation—troubles, heartaches, and pains. These are they—men and women, boys and girls, Black and White, rich and poor, able and disabled, in homes and homeless—who have kept the faith, washed their robes in the blood of the Lamb. These are they who walk beside the spring of living water with the assurance that God will wipe away all tears from our eyes. These are they who approach the throne of God's saving grace. We must, however, keep our faith and keep on working with the assurance that God knows all about us and is able to keep us safe in all situations. After all, as the song says, it will "soon be over and we'll shout Hallelujah, by and by." Keep the faith. God has a plan for our lives.

Suggestions for Worship

Call to Worship

LEADER: Praise the Lord, all nations! Bless the Lord, all people!

PEOPLE: **Give God the glory for in wisdom God guides our feet in a land of plenty.**

LEADER: Praise the Lord, my sisters! Bless the Lord, my brothers!

PEOPLE: **Give thanks to God for honor is due to the one who restores our souls and leads us in the paths of righteousness.**

LEADER: Praise the Lord, children! Bless the Lord, elders!

PEOPLE: **Power and might belong to the one who even in our darkest** moments walks with us and protects us from hurt, harm, and danger.

LEADER: Praise the Lord, church! Bless the Lord, believers!

PEOPLE: **God invites each of us to the table of honor and makes our enemies our footstools.**

ALL: **Praise the Lord, everybody, for God sends goodness and mercy all the days of our lives and invites us to dwell in the new "kin-dom" forever and ever. Amen.**

Prayer of Confession

"God of our weary years, God of our silent tears,"[1] God of patience and hope, we come before your presence as empty vessels, waiting to be filled with your life-giving power. Lord, you have loved us when we could not love ourselves, when we listened to other voices and didn't remember who you told us you were. Lord, as we grow in grace, we are learning to listen to your voice and hear you call our names. We realize that if we keep our hearts and minds stayed on you and our hand in your unchanging hand that no one can harm us, no one can snatch us out of your presence. Lord, we love you and pray that you will enable us to respect all creation and remember daily who and whose we are. Amen.

Sending Forth

Send us out, Lord, dressed in the whole armor of God, engaging the evils of this world that would knock us out, down, or in.

Send us out, Lord, empowered to tell a dying world that we all can live because you live in us. Amen.

———————

1. James Weldon Johnson, "Lift Every Voice and Sing," Edward B. Marks Music Co., copyright 1921, renewed.

Fifth Sunday of Easter

Agnes W. Norfleet

Acts 11:1-18: Peter recounts his vision in Joppa, he speaks to a gathering of Gentiles, and the Spirit falls upon them.

Psalm 148: All creation is summoned to praise the Lord.

Revelation 21:1-6: John sees the holy city coming down out of heaven and hears God's promises to wipe away tears and abolish death, crying, and pain.

John 13:31-35: Jesus gives a new commandment—"that you love one another."

REFLECTIONS

It is amazing what a person will say to a pregnant woman. *What to Expect When You're Expecting* and all the other books about pregnancy warn us about this phenomenon—how complete strangers will join you on an elevator and put a hand on your belly; how someone will try to convince you you're having twins when you're only five or six months along. And it's true; it happens; I am amazed at what people will say.

The most memorable comments from my second pregnancy came from that marvelous international community, the Dekalb Farmers Market. Two cashiers, a man and a woman, got into a conversation about whether I was going to have a boy or a girl. You know, everyone thinks he or she can tell by the way you carry the baby. They got so excited in the debate that they left the English language and continued in Hindi. I made that assumption because that's what their name tags indicated they spoke. I could have easily settled that debate, but I didn't know how to say "amniocentesis" in Hindi. So I just smiled, paid for my groceries, and went home.

But I had a more poignant conversation a couple of weeks later in the same market. I was comparing the prices of apples and deciding between apples and pears. A woman standing next to me said, "Is this your first child?" "No, I have a little boy who's almost two," I replied. And then she said, not with a smile but with a grave expression, "How can you dare to bring children into this cruel and terrible world?" I went back to my decision about the apples and pears, but I've got to admit the question stung. I understand what she meant.

A SERMON BRIEF

The world has never been completely safe for children, but there is a sadness in knowing that even the world I grew up in was safer than the world into which our children are being born.

As a young child I had free reign of a large city block and a wooded area to build forts in. As a teenager I could pedal my bike as far away from home as my legs would take me. As a young person I was well into my college years before I ever smelled marijuana or knew that somebody knew that so-and-so's roommate probably did drugs. I know that our children will have less freedom and more exposure than I ever could have imagined. Our world is indeed a dangerous place for children.

In the spring of 1995 I remember talking with a member of the congregation about being deeply moved by the commemorations of the end of World War II in Europe. Sharing a similar reaction, she said that she heard one commentator on television saying that the victory in Europe was the last time we really felt good about ourselves as a nation. There was then a sense that with the fall of Hitler and the German forces a powerful evil had been defeated. That part of the war was over, and we rejoiced. The victory over Japan did not carry the same good feeling because we had unleashed such terrible power in the atomic bomb. The victory in Europe was the last time we felt good about ourselves as a nation.

I imagine that in the spring of 1995 many of us watched the celebrations for the fiftieth anniversary of the end of World War II with a certain anxiety about today's world. In black and white the documentaries showed filmed footage of the concentration camps being freed, and in living color the evening news showed armed Serb soldiers separating men from women and children and driving them away in buses. In black and white the documentaries showed beleaguered Russian troops stumbling home in the mud, and in living color the evening news showed the Chechen civilian houses being fired upon. In black and white the American and French soldiers partied down the Champs-Elysees, and in living color the Michigan militia marched to an anti-American tune. Perhaps all of us parents and would-be parents should ask ourselves, "How do we dare to bring children into this cruel and terrible world?"

Our scripture readings find us in an era of uncertainty, a sort of in-between time. In the Gospel of John, Jesus is giving farewell instructions to perplexed disciples before his departure. They cling to Jesus as if hanging on for dear life. "Little children," Jesus says, "I am with you only a little longer. You will look for me . . . where I am going you cannot come. . . ." Then he tells them how to live when he leaves: "Love one another . . . just as I have loved you."

Those disciples may have wondered if their presence in the company of Jesus would be the last time that they would feel good about themselves. Jesus was trying to let them know that the end of his life would inaugurate the beginning of a new creation. With Jesus' earthly departure what would hold them together as a community was a dramatic persistent love like the love Jesus had for them.

The poet, writer, and prophet James Baldwin wrote:

One must say Yes to life and embrace it wherever it is found—and it is found in terrible places. . . . For nothing is fixed, forever and forever and forever, it is not fixed; the earth is always shifting, the light is always changing, the sea does not cease to grind down rock. Generations do not cease to be born, and we are responsible to them because we are the only witnesses they have. The sea rises, the light fails, lovers cling to each other, and children cling to us. The moment we cease to hold each other, the moment we break faith with one another, the sea engulfs us and the light goes out. (Richard Avedon and James Baldwin, *Nothing Personal* [New York: Dell, 1965], section 4.)

"James Baldwin left the church of his childhood and youth because of the abusive and inflexible attitudes of his minister father and others; but, thankfully, Baldwin never lost his sense of connectedness with other human beings, even those in the church. The titles of many of his writings are taken from his African-American spiritual tradition" (Rush Otey, "Protagonist Corner: An Invitation to I Thessalonians," *Journal for Preachers* 18:4 [Pentecost 1995], 40). And, even though he may have left the church, he never gave up on the impassioned plea of Jesus to his disciples: Even though I am leaving, Jesus says, don't break faith with one another, and hold fast together in love.

We live in an in-between time, between the departure of Jesus' earthly ministry and the fulfillment of God's new creation. We look back at John's Gospel, and we see Jesus, who taught us how to live, who showed us how to love, and who promised a new life in his name. We look forward to the Revelation of John, and we see a future cradled in the loving hands of God—a new heaven, a new earth, a new Jerusalem.

The philosopher Friedrich Nietzsche said, "Love is the state in which [one] sees things most widely different from what they are." In this cruel and terrible world, that is the calling of Christians—to love by seeing things differently from what they are; in other words, to live by the vision God holds before us. God knows our lives will be shaped by what we see. "See, the home of God is among mortals. [God] will dwell with them; they will be [God's] peoples, and . . . [God] will wipe every tear from their eyes. Death will be no more; mourning and crying and pain will be no more. . . . See, I am making all things new."

Throughout the book of Revelation God has been pictured as mysterious, majestic, and victorious. Now God is pictured as wiping away tears from the eyes of children. This is a great promise that the painful experiences of this world will be overcome. Our future is cradled in the care and concern and comfort of God's love.

How do I dare to bring children into this cruel and terrible world? I see the world as it is. I also have a vision of what the world will be.

SUGGESTIONS FOR WORSHIP

Call to Worship

Psalm 148 could be read antiphonally.

Prayer of Confession (based on John 13:34; Acts 11:1-18)

O Lord, forgive us, for we your disciples have not loved one another. We have drawn distinctions among us. We have missed your visions that would open us to new understandings of your ways in the world. We have missed your messengers who would open us to new relationships with others and with your Spirit. Most especially we have not loved others as you loved us. Love us still and transform us, that everyone may know we are your disciples because of our love for one another. Amen.

Benediction

May the Alpha and the Omega, the Beginning and the End, grant you grace to keep faith with one another and to hold fast together in love.

Ascension Day

Barbara Shires Blaisdell

Acts 1:1-11: The story of Jesus' ascension includes two promises: the gift of the Holy Spirit and the eventual return of Jesus.

Psalm 47: "Clap your hands, all you peoples. . . . God has gone up with a shout."

Ephesians 1:15-23: Paul tells the Christians at Ephesus that he gives thanks for them constantly in his prayers. He also prays that they may know "what is the hope to which [God] has called you" and "what is the immeasurable greatness of [God's] power . . . and [God] has put all things under [Christ's] feet."

Luke 24:44-53: The closing verses of the Gospel tell of Jesus' ascension. He opens the disciples' minds to understand Scripture, calls them "witnesses," promises them "power from on high," and is "carried up into heaven."

REFLECTIONS

Today's text is another one of those strange stories that Steven Spielberg would love to direct, filled with special effects of shadow and light. I picture him setting the scene high on a rugged mountain, with vivid blue Mediterranean sky in the background, the musical score vaguely Middle Eastern and mysterious, swelling to crescendo as the sky darkens. And Jesus, in the spotlight, slowly levitates like a giant helium balloon being filled on the eve of the Macy's Thanksgiving Day parade. All eyes follow him up, up, up into the heavens.

Now this is problematic and awkward for those of us who no longer believe that heaven is literally "up there." We still use that language but we use it symbolically. We know because we've sent astronauts up there, and we realize that heaven is not a certain elevation in the sky. If pressed to go beyond our symbolic language, most of us would speak of heaven as another dimension altogether. Or we'd speak of heaven as that time/space event in which God's will is finally and fully done. Heaven is where God exists in fullness and where we find our completeness, our wholeness, all we are destined in God to become.

The good news for us postmodern, post-space travel people is that Luke does not paint that picture of Jesus as a holy, helium balloon. His language is much more simple. He does speak of Christ's being lifted. He speaks of Christ's blessing them. He says something about a cloud that covers him or takes him from their sight. And when Christ is gone, the disciples stand, staring up into empty sky. And two strangers are standing by them to say with far too little fanfare, "Why are you looking up there? He will come back some day."

A SERMON BRIEF

The ancient church associated a psalm with the ascension, Psalm 47:

> Clap your hands, all you peoples;
>   shout to God with loud songs of joy.
> For the LORD, the Most High, is awesome,
>   a great king over all the earth.

That language describing the power and authority of God is the language of elevation. The psalmist continues: "God has gone up with a shout. . . ." The ancient church heard that language and said that those words sound like what we believe about Christ. We no longer hear his voice. But we sense his presence nevertheless. We sense that Christ is over us all.

Why do we need to say that?

Most people in the world would say that there is a sovereign power over us all. The question is: What kind of power? What kind of God? An angry, temperamental God? An imperious, controlling God, pulling strings in order to watch us dance painfully on the end of those strings like marionettes? An impassive, inaccessible God?

The Hebrew Scriptures represent an attempt to wade through those options: What kind of God? And the Christian doctrine of the Ascension centers us right in the middle of the best of those scriptures: ours is a God who loves and who commands love. It is this God of love that Christ reveals and ascends to join on the throne of heaven.

It would be easier if he had not gone. If he were here, we could ask him face-to-face who is right about all the important disagreements of the church. We could ask him our toughest questions—all that stuff he didn't get around to in the Gospels. Of course, we assume we'd like the answers. But even if we didn't, we could accommodate ourselves to them if we just knew for sure. And what a comfort it would be just to see the face of the one we follow or to talk to someone who saw his face last week. But this is not to be. We are required to be more adult than that.

Augustine said that Christ departed from our eyes so that we should return to our own hearts and find him there. No wonder the disciples stood staring into the sky. We'd all rather look into the sky rather than into our own hearts. It requires too much responsibility to look inside. Which is why we are so tempted to revert to something physical and external. We—all of us—turn to our favorite parts of the Bible and project on them an unambiguous simplicity that they don't have. We elevate them to a status they do not claim, breathe a sigh of relief, and say, "Well now, that issue is settled." Or we do the same kind of projection toward people or systems—looking to something solid, external, physical in which to place our trust.

Instead we have this Christ whom we cannot hold or touch. Instead we have the memory and teachings of this Jesus of Nazareth and all that we have seen in him: his earthiness, his affection for children, his tears, his compassion, his fury with hypocrisy and dishonest pride, his patience with us who are so slow to learn the power, the magnificent power of suffering love. We have this Christ. And this, the Ascension says, more than anything else is the power that has risen over all things, including our own hearts. So clap your hands, all you peoples. Shout to God with loud songs of joy. For the Lord, most High, is awesome. This is the power above all the universe.

But what if you don't feel like clapping? What if you've looked up into the sky and seen not Christ but only clouds? We would be fools not to acknowledge that sin is strong and hate is powerful and evil is real. But the promise of the Ascension is that mercy is mightier. Grace is greater. Love will lure all toward its promise. No matter who is shouting the loudest now, love will have the final word. The news we've got is not that everything has been made all right already—not by a long shot. The news we've been given is that the ultimate outcome has been promised. What we know is whose hands hold the whole world. But the world is not finished even inside those mighty hands. The world is not finished with all its rebellions, its refusals to love and be loved. The troubles and the tears are not over, and there is no completely satisfactory answer to the question why. We do know that God created us and others in a freedom that can be triumphant or terrible, a freedom to be creative or chaotic, a freedom to dream dreams, and an equal freedom to destruct and take others with us. It is a freedom offered not only to our souls but to the very cells within us and to all the other billions and billions of cells out there. If you are caught up in the terrible chaotic, destructive side of freedom, either of your own making or a chaos imposed by the freedom of others, if you are struggling because you can't see much evidence that love commands this world, if you are having trouble trusting that anything will be all right in the end, this text invites you to remember the patient, gentle love of Christ.

It is true that some signs of the full sovereignty of God we must wait for. But a huge part can be settled right now, even at this very moment. Who will reign as sovereign in your life? There are many gods who would reign over our living. Anxiety wants to reign. Ego wants to reign. Money wants sovereignty. The company wants it. Our anger wants it. Some days despair wants it. What is it that has ascended over your life and mine, ruling all that we are and all that we do? May it be this patient, long-suffering, luring love that is ours in Christ Jesus.

SUGGESTIONS FOR WORSHIP

Call to Worship (Psalm 47 adapted)

LEADER: Clap your hands, all you peoples. Shout to God with songs of joy.

PEOPLE: **For the Lord our God is awesome, a great ruler over all the earth.**

LEADER: God has gone up with a shout; sing praises to God; sing praises.

PEOPLE: **Sing praises to God; sing praises. For God rules over all. God sits on the holy throne.**

Prayer of Confession

Ruler of the universe,
You who spin planets and plant stars,
You who create the seen and guide the unseen,
You who scatter the proud and welcome the sinner,

We worship you this morning with all your creation.
With needs and thanks crowding our hearts,
   we gather before your throne.
Hear now our silent prayers of confession . . .
Forgive us in the name of Jesus Christ, we pray. Amen.

Assurance of Pardon (Luke 24:46-48 adapted)

"Thus it is written, that the Messiah is to suffer and to rise from the dead on the third day, and that repentance and forgiveness of sins is to be proclaimed in his name to all nations, beginning here . . . You are witnesses of these things." Friends, believe the good news. In Jesus Christ we are forgiven.

Benediction

You women and men of ————, why stand ye gazing upward? "You will receive power," Jesus said, "after the Holy Spirit has come upon you. And you will be my witnesses . . . ."

Go out into the world in peace. And may the grace of Christ embolden you, the love of God enfold you, the Holy Spirit empower you, now and forevermore. Amen.

Day of Pentecost

Charlotte McGruder Abram

Genesis 11:1-9: The people of the earth, all speaking the same language, conspire to reach the heavens by human efforts. Motivated by pride ("let us make a name for ourselves," v. 4*b*) and seeking security through unity ("otherwise we shall be scattered abroad" v. 4*c*), they build a high tower. To prevent the escalation and recurrence of their arrogant efforts, God confuses their language and scatters them abroad.

Psalm 104:24-34, 35*b*: "O LORD, how manifold are your works! In wisdom you have made them all. . . . "

Acts 2:1-21: Gathered together, the disciples await the promised coming of "power from on high" (Luke 24:49). With the sound of rushing wind, and a touch from tongues of fire, the Holy Spirit fills believers. Empowered by the Spirit, disciples speak "about God's deeds of power" (v. 11*b*) in the languages of the diverse world community gathered outside its door. Some amazed observers suggest believers are drunk. Peter says Not so, this is the fulfillment of the prophecy of Joel.

John 14:8-17, (25-27): Jesus promises not to abandon his disciples when he returns to heaven. God will send an "Advocate . . . the Spirit of truth" (vv. 16-17), who will abide with them and in them. This "Advocate, the Holy Spirit" (v. 26), will teach them and remind them of all Jesus said. This assurance is given to allay fears and leave them with inner peace.

REFLECTIONS

At a church-based community organizing meeting, one woman became frustrated with the tedious attention being given to organizational details. She raised her hand and said, "I thought this meeting was about taking the gospel to the streets?"

Pentecost, often called the birthday of the church, does not celebrate the birth of an organization. Pentecost is the story of how the church came alive by the power of the Holy Spirit. On that day followers of Jesus Christ received the power to take the gospel to the streets there in Jerusalem and eventually throughout the earth.

On that day a mighty wind from heaven blew the fire of the Holy Spirit into those followers who were gathered together. It blew into them a sense of boldness. It blew into them an awareness that, just as Jesus had promised, the presence of the Holy Spirit was with them and now at work in and through them. The sound that came from heaven, that rushing violent wind, was the exciting sound of old barriers being broken and glass ceilings shattering. The divisions within humanity, as characterized by the different languages, were overcome. The preconceived patriarchal notion that God's call to prophesy is restricted to the male gender was toppled. The church, unencumbered by human limitations, took to the streets with an inclusive message.

The Holy Spirit is still in the business of filling us with the boldness to respond to those who question . . . still in the business of helping us break down barriers and build bridges . . . still in the business of spreading the word that "everyone who calls on the name of the Lord shall be saved" (Acts 2:21). That business is called "The Church."

A SERMON BRIEF

Dr. Zan Holmes, professor of homiletics at Perkins School of Theology, tells the story of a young man who was sitting on a park bench next to the young woman he liked. They sat in silence for a long time until finally the young woman said, "Well, aren't you going to say something?" The young man replied, "I was just sitting here thinking." The young woman asked, "You're just sitting here thinking about what?" He said, "I was just sitting here thinking and wishing I was an octopus." She asked, "Why would you want to be an octopus?" He replied, "Well, if I were an octopus, I'd have eight arms and I could hug you and squeeze you with all eight of my arms." The young woman said, "Huh! You don't have to be an octopus with eight arms to hug and squeeze me. You ain't doing nothing with the two good arms you got!" That young man lacked the power to make an effective witness.

Likewise, the disciples, after Jesus' arrest and before the day of Pentecost, lacked the power to witness about the redeeming love of God.

The Gospel of John paints a picture of the disciples hiding behind locked doors following the death and resurrection of Jesus (John 20:19). Fear had stripped them of the power to witness. Yet the disciples were not alone. Most all of us at one time or another have lacked the power to witness, haven't we? Perhaps we've been in the company of people who tell jokes that have subtle racist or sexist undertones or demean others. We let the moment pass without reply. We have the words of challenge and truth on our tongues and yet we swallow them unspoken. We, too, sometimes lack the power to witness to our beliefs and values.

When we lack the power to witness, the problem for us is the same problem the first disciples faced. William Willimon suggests that the challenge the first disciples faced was not that of knowing about Jesus. They could tell people all the facts about Jesus. Facts were not enough. They needed the authorization and empowerment that would enable them and all witnesses after them to not only talk about what Jesus did, but to do what Jesus did.[1] Through the Spirit's power, they would be able to walk the walk as well as talk the talk.

On the day of Pentecost the disciples acquired a holy boldness they had never had before. The difference in them after Pentecost was as dramatic as those before-and-after pictures that weight loss programs advertise. Before Pentecost, on the night of Jesus' arrest, Peter cowers away from a servant girl's inquiry and refuses to admit that he knew Jesus (Luke 22:56-57). But look who's talking now. After Pentecost, it is Peter who speaks to the confused and questioning crowd. It is Peter who boldly proclaims the fulfillment of the prophecy of Joel. The Spirit gives him the power to witness to the devout crowd of Jews, who "know the Scriptures, [but] do not see what the Scripture so clearly proved."[2] Today there is still a devout crowd, who know the Scripture but can't as yet see what Scripture affirms. Yet, as with the first disciples, the Holy Spirit has given us the power to witness to that devout crowd, too.

A family in my parish asked me to conduct the funeral service for their oldest daughter. This young woman, who had lived out-of-town most of her adult life, had been a high school and college classmate of mine. She was well known and loved in our community. On the day of the service, my stomach was tied in knots. I was nervous because this was only the third funeral I had ever preached. I was nervous because I had never conducted a funeral of a friend or someone my own age. Most of all, I was nervous because I cared deeply and identified closely with this family. I asked God to give me the ability to bring them a word of comfort in this time of sorrow.

The service was being held at a neighboring Baptist church because our building couldn't accommodate the crowd. The church's pastor, who was not bound by tradition, offered full use of the church. I stepped into the pulpit, realizing that I was probably the first woman preacher to have ever stood there. The pastors of several other family members were present in support of this well-known family. Consequently, behind me sat another Baptist pastor, a Lutheran pastor, and a Catholic priest. They were, I'm sure, taken aback when they realized that a woman was delivering the sermon.

Toward the end of the preaching the Holy Spirit took over that service. As I began proclaiming our hope in the Resurrection, several family members stood and began praising God. The outpouring of the Holy Spirit allowed all of us to experience true joy in the time of sorrow. And even those who doubted the validity of a woman preacher had to concede later that the Spirit had been poured out and a maidservant did prophesy. By the power of the Holy Spirit we, too, are able to walk the walk and talk the talk that gives witness to the powerful way in which the Spirit has been poured out on all flesh.

When the Holy Spirit came with a mighty wind from heaven and tongues of fire, the disciples came alive with the power to witness to those both inside and outside their faith community. They had the power to speak in the languages of the people who were in the streets right outside their door. More than ever before, the crowds right outside our church doors need to hear and experience the powerful Word of God in a language they can understand.

In his book, *The Kingdom of God Is a Party* (Waco, Tex.: Word, 1990), Tony Campolo tells of a time when he spoke in Honolulu. Because of the time difference between Hawaii and the mainland, Campolo was wide awake and hungry at 3:30 in the morning. He went out in search of a restaurant that was still open and found a little "greasy spoon" diner. As he sat finishing his coffee, several women came in who had just gotten off work. He knew they were prostitutes. He kept drinking his coffee as they sat on each side of him, talking. Finally one young woman mentioned to her companion that tomorrow was her birthday. The companion responded sarcastically that that wasn't so special and then hinted that the first woman only mentioned it so someone would throw her a birthday party. The first woman replied that she didn't expect to get something from her companion; in fact, she'd never even had a birthday party. She just wanted someone to know that tomorrow was her birthday.

After the women left, Campolo found out from the diner's owner, Harry, that these women came to the diner every night at the same hour, and that the woman celebrating a birthday was named Agnes. Campolo then asked Harry if he would help set up a birthday party for Agnes. Harry agreed.

Early the following morning, the diner was filled with party decorations when several women—even more than the morning before—began coming in off the street. When Agnes came in, everyone sang "Happy Birthday" to her. She was so overjoyed that when the cake with candles arrived, she started crying and had to have Harry blow the candles out for her. When it came time to cut the cake, Agnes begged to take the cake home to admire.

After Agnes left, proudly carrying the cake, Campolo led the group in prayer for Agnes and the other women. When he finished, Harry said that he didn't know Campolo was a preacher and asked the type of church at which he preached. Campolo replied that it was a church that gives birthday parties for prostitutes, the church of Jesus Christ.

That church is here to apply the healing salve of the gospel to the woundedness in our souls as we proclaim that salvation is available to all. That church today, praise God, is alive, with the power to witness!

Suggestions for Worship

Call to Worship

LEADER: Come, believers and faithful ones, sing your alleluias to God!

PEOPLE: **Praise God, who invades us with the rush of a mighty wind and fills us with fire.**

LEADER: Praise God, who out of love for us sent Jesus Christ to live among us.

PEOPLE: **Praise God, whose spirit is poured out upon all flesh so our sons and daughters might prophesy.**

LEADER: God reaches into our lives and claims us, calling us honored and loved.

PEOPLE: **We are God's people: We are redeemed; for God has called us by name.**

ALL: **Come, Holy Spirit, and find us in our wilderness. Lead us forth into the wonders of your love.**

(Jann C. Weaver in *Flames of the Spirit,* edited by Ruth C. Duck [New York: Pilgrim Press, 1985], p. 46). Reprinted with the permission of The Pilgrim Press.

Prayer of Confession (based on Gen. 11:1-8; Acts 2:1-21)

Dear Gracious Loving God,
We confess that oftentimes we come to you seeking our will and our way. We have a program plan for the church and we want you to bless it. Yet outside of your will, even our best efforts lead to confusion and disunity. Erase every agenda that is rooted in prideful arrogance. Forgive us, touch us, fill and empower us. By the power of the Holy Spirit, set us loose in the world to witness to all people everywhere your powerful deeds of love. Amen.

Assurance of Pardon

Good news. The Holy Spirit is in our midst, forgiving, renewing and empowering us. In the name of Jesus Christ your are forgiven.

Sending Forth

The Spirit has been poured out on all flesh. Let us go now, on fire with God's love, embodying the message of salvation for all, building gracious communities of peace, hope and unity.

---

1. William H. Willimon, *Acts. Interpretation, A Bible Commentary for Teaching and Preaching* (Atlanta: John Knox, 1988).
2. Ibid., p. 35.

Ordinary Time 15 or Proper 10

Ann L. Petker

Amos 7:7-17: The passage begins with one of a series of visions. Verses 7-9 describe God's coming judgment on the people. Verses 10-17 contain biographical information about the prophet Amos.

Psalm 82: In this profession of faith, God passes judgment against the other gods of ancient polytheism. With their guilt established, God's just reign is instituted.

Colossians 1:1-14: A letter of thanksgiving and encouragement to the Colossian church.

Luke 10:25-37: The well-known parable of the good Samaritan.

REFLECTIONS

As a wife, mother, and friend, I have held fast to the importance of writing loving notes and letters to those I care about. As a pastor, I am constantly filled with the desire to let my congregation know how much they are loved by God. I was struck by the passage from Colossians because it is a love letter written to a congregation reminding them of what God has done for them—because God loves them so much. This text so wonderfully sums up the essence of our faith while calling the church to claim the power that comes from God through Jesus Christ. It allows us as preachers to eloquently proclaim to our congregations the life-changing love of God. We can, none of us, women or men, hear too often how much we are loved.

A Sermon Brief

True confession. I am a dyed-in-the-wool, true romantic. I love dinners by candlelight, weekends away, small notes bearing loving affirmations turning up in my suitcase when I am on a trip, flowers arriving at my door, phone calls just to say "I love you." The occurrence of any one of these will absolutely make my day. There is something else, too, that has the power to make me feel all mushy and warm inside: a love song. For years now, I have delighted in trying to keep up with the latest the music world has to offer in love songs. I learn the words of my favorite ones, singing aloud in full voice when no one is around to hear me. Along with the words, I remember the pain of long lost loves and celebrate the fullness of the love I share with my husband, Allan. There is something about a good love song that fills my heart and reminds me of the power of love.

The opening lines of the letter to the Colossians are followed by verses that are part of an early hymn or poem. Together, they form a love song that speaks to the very heart of our faith, celebrating the great love of God-made-flesh, Jesus Christ. Like any love song, this song speaks of heartache as well as triumph. There will be painful times, it reminds us, but we can enter those times in confidence, knowing that we will receive power from the One who has already overcome the darkness on our behalf.

"He has rescued us from the power of darkness. . . ."

She wasn't very old, just a young girl growing up in a household that is far too common in our society today—a house of broken relationships, full of fear. Fear of the all-too-frequent rages. Fear of tirades, of verbal and physical abuse. She grew up afraid. She grew up thinking she wasn't very valuable or talented, and she kept all of the abuse a buried secret. But she vowed that she would never treat her children the way she had been treated, that although the statistics said that she, too, would grow up to be an abuser, that she would most likely have unhappy relationships, she promised herself she would be different. Many years later this young girl is a grown woman, in a long and happy marriage, with children whom she has never abused. She has created a beautiful home and is in ministry caring for others, sharing with them the transforming power and love of Jesus Christ.

"He has rescued us from the power of darkness. . . ."

They had been married for several years and had two children. They were very active in their church. This couple struggled in their marriage. The husband was abusive emotionally. Finally the wife said she wanted a divorce, and they separated. One evening the husband came to the house to plead with her not to continue with the divorce proceedings. When his wife did not change her mind, he got up abruptly and went outside. She didn't know where he had gone. She looked out the window just in time to see him pulling a gun out of the front seat of his car. Returning to the house, he kicked in the door and, shoving the gun in her face, threatened to kill her if she did not agree to stop the divorce proceedings. The husband ended up holding both his wife and small son at gunpoint for the next four hours. When he finally left, he was picked up quickly by the police. Word of what had occurred reached the church. After the wife discussed her situation with church leaders, she was told that if she divorced her husband she could not stay at the church. So she left the church. Many years later she is remarried, she has rebuilt her life, she has found happiness, she has taken training to be an advocate for other victims of domestic violence.

"He has rescued us from the power of darkness. . . ."

The other night I was engaged in a theological discussion with my sixteen-year-old son, Joshua. His questions were those which people have asked through the ages searching for an understanding of the Christian faith. As I pondered our conversation later, it all seemed to filter down to one word . . . *Why?* Why God, why did Jesus have to die? Why? I felt woefully inadequate to fully give the answer to his whys. Then I reread this scripture passage, this hymn of praise, this love song, and I realized afresh that it was not my words, no matter how wise, that would bring my son to a full understanding of God. There are no words that can put faith in someone else's heart, only a personal encounter with Jesus Christ can do that.

"He has rescued us from the power of darkness. . . ."

A pastor friend recently shared with me an experience she had when she attended her denomination's annual conference. The gathering occurred at a church that had begun four years earlier with twelve charter members and their pastor. At the start, the host pastor walked out in front of her colleagues and said, "I just want to say to you, I love Jesus Christ. So when you meet people and they say to you, 'What is she like?' you can say to them, 'She is passionately in love with Jesus Christ.' " This woman had had a personal encounter with Jesus Christ. It had made an incredible difference in her life. That's the kind of experience that gives birth to faith in a sixteen-year-old boy and gives a young girl hope. That's the kind of experience that makes it possible for a young mother to face down a gun barrel or a board of elders.

It's this kind of experience and this Jesus Christ that our scripture celebrates today. God wrote the love song, and through the song God reaches out and touches us personally, bringing us close. The Spirit whispers the song into our hearts, and we are invited to sing the song of love, to be changed by the song, to share the song joyfully and boldly.

Why, Joshua? I cannot explain love to you. I will never be able to describe the love I have felt for you from the very first moment I laid eyes on you and how every year that love has continued to grow. Someday maybe you will be a parent and then you will understand. I cannot clearly define for you what it feels like to fall in love with the person who is to become your life partner, your best friend. It's impossible to describe how you know when someone is the one whom you want to spend your life with. Someday maybe you will know the joy of falling in love with the right person and then you will understand. It is impossible to describe love with words alone. You need to listen with your heart as well.

Why Jesus, Joshua? I cannot explain to you with words alone how deeply I love Jesus. I cannot explain to you with words alone how deeply I know Jesus loves me and you. I cannot define my absolute confidence that we are resting in his care, that he does make me strong with the strength that comes from his glorious power, that he has allowed me to endure many difficult things, confident that he would rescue me from the power of darkness and transfer me into the light of his kingdom. But I know. I pray that you, too, will hear the love song. Listen with your heart. He is singing to you. His song will change your life.

SUGGESTIONS FOR WORSHIP

Call to Worship

LEADER: Let us rejoice in God;

PEOPLE: **For God makes us strong, with God's glorious power.**

LEADER: Let us rejoice in God;

PEOPLE: **For God enables us to share in the inheritance of the saints in the light.**

LEADER: Let us rejoice in God;

PEOPLE: **For God has rescued us from the power of darkness.**

ALL: **Let us worship the God of our salvation who has transferred us into the kingdom of Jesus Christ, through whom we have been forgiven of our sins.**

Prayer of Confession

God of love, forgive us when we turn from you and your will for our lives. We easily forget your great love for us, and all you have done for us. Open our hearts to receive your love, that with joy we may celebrate our salvation and share your Good News with all the world. Amen.

Assurance of Pardon

Hear the good news: God's love for us has no limits. Because of that love, we have been forgiven through Jesus Christ. Let us celebrate the gift of new life!

Benediction (based on Col. 1:11-14)

May you be made strong with all the strength that comes from God's glorious power, joyfully giving thanks to God who has redeemed us through Jesus Christ.

Ordinary Time 20 or Proper 15

Mary Cartledge-Hayes

Hosea 11:1-11: Earlier verses have depicted the punishment coming because of Israel's disobedience, but hope remains. God was once "like those who lift infants to their cheek." Even now, God's compassion will continue.

Psalm 107:1-9, 43: The theme of this psalm of thanksgiving is appreciation for God's steadfast love, as demonstrated in God's saving action in rescuing those who "wandered in desert wastes."

Colossians 3:1-11: Paul describes life for those who "have been raised with Christ." He admonishes believers to "put on the new nature" and reminds them that divisions can no longer exist, because "Christ is all, and in all."

Luke 12:13-21: A listener asks Jesus for help in getting a piece of his brother's inheritance. Jesus replies with the parable of the foolish rich man who worries about how to store his wealth, unaware that he will die in the night.

REFLECTIONS

An abiding issue for preachers is how to preach to the whole congregation. In today's passage the specific question is how to include women's reality while preaching on a passage with a decidedly masculine cast. All the characters are male: younger brother, older brother, rich man, and Jesus. The questions raised and answered in the text (How do I get my hands on an inheritance? How are we to handle wealth?) while not specific to men, certainly come up more frequently for men than for women. After all, the adage is still true: most women are only one paycheck away from poverty. So we have male actors and a topic—hoarding wealth—that many women don't lose much sleep over. What, then, is the message of the passage, the essence that transcends financial, gender, and social differences?

The answer lies in its warning against letting concern for material possessions be the center of our existence. Greed—focusing on the overabundance of material possessions to the point that nothing else matters—is one side of the coin. The other side of the coin is focusing on an underabundance of material possessions to the point that nothing else matters. In both situations, God is overlooked, left out entirely, or used to explain financial circumstance (i.e., wealth shows one is living in God's favor; poverty proves one is out of favor). Jesus' teaching makes clear that money is not the acceptable center of our existence; God is.

A SERMON BRIEF

On August 6, 1945, the United States dropped a bomb on the city of Hiroshima, Japan. A writer named John Hersey wrote about what he saw in a park in Hiroshima that day ("The Day the Bomb Fell," *The New Yorker,* July 31, 1995, pp. 65-67, excerpted from "Hiroshima," *The New Yorker,* 1946). The park was far enough away from the explosion that its trees— bamboo, pine, laurel, and maple—were still leafy and green after the blast. Hersey says people streamed into the park. They came because they thought if more bombs fell, they would drop on buildings, not in a park. They came because the park felt safe and normal to them. They came, too, he said, because of an irresistible urge to hide under leaves.

Hersey says among the people were a group of priests. A theological student was with them. The student had packed two pairs of shoes with his clothing, but the package had come loose and all that remained were two left shoes. He went off looking for the two right shoes, and found one. When he came back, he said, "It's funny, but things don't matter anymore. Yesterday, my shoes were my most important possessions. Today, I don't care. One pair is enough."

The man who questioned Jesus in today's reading is unhappy. He is a younger brother, his father has died, and he wants a portion of the inheritance. It's as though all he has is one pair of shoes, and it's not enough. He wants more. He's decided Jesus is wise and fair, and he wants some of that fairness to be applied to him. The younger brother is asking Jesus to judge what is his fair share.

In response Jesus tells a parable that doesn't seem to apply to the younger brother at all. His parable isn't about a younger brother; it's about the one who has it all, the rich man who seems to have everything.

The rich man is not a bad man. Jesus doesn't say he's unjust, that he underpays his workers or stiffs his creditors. He's a fortunate man, fortunate that sun and rain have come at the right time and in the right measure so that he's had abundant crops. But this fortunate man doesn't appreciate what's been given to him. He frets over what to do with it and how to hang on to it. He is, in the words of God, a fool, greedy for the treasures of earth rather than for the treasures of God.

After telling the parable, Jesus basically says, "You people fret yourselves about what you have or don't have or might have or might lose. Now why would you do that?" And then he goes on to talk of things that seem trivial: birds and wildflowers, ravens and lilies.

I actually saw a flock of ravens awhile back. Until then, I thought the reference to ravens was about some sweet birds you'd watch sweeping through the sky at dusk, like the songbirds that perched on the telephone wires when I was growing up, who chirped and sang and held conversations among themselves. Then I saw and heard a flock of ravens. Ravens are spooky birds, over two feet long, big and squat, blue-black with a long hooked bill, fierce. They don't perch prettily. They don't sing sweetly, even though they are songbirds. You wouldn't really even call the noise they make a squawk. It's deeper and louder. It makes a chill run up your spine and back down. They're the birds of which nightmares are made, or poetry by Edgar Allan Poe.

Ravens don't work in the fields. They don't tuck their food for winter away in barns, either. God feeds them. And you, says Jesus, are more valuable to God than the ravens. So why are you anxious about your possessions?

And now let's think about the lilies. The image I see is from the old movie *Doctor Zhivago*. There are fields and fields and fields of daffodils stretching as far as the eye can see. *Doctor Zhivago* is a dark, brooding movie set in Russia in the winter. It is the kind of movie in which I nod off after the first fifteen minutes. But I was awake for that one brief moment when all you can see are the yellows and greens of daffodils in full bloom, stretching into eternity.

Solomon in all his glory, says Jesus, was not clothed as beautifully as one daffodil or one lily. Solomon in all his glory couldn't match one wildflower that blooms today and fades tomorrow.

Lilies don't spin fiber into fabric. They don't toil at all. And yet they are clothed better than the richest king. And you, says Jesus, are more valuable to God than the lilies. So why are you anxious about your possessions?

God knows what you need, says Jesus. You don't have to strive after possessions. Strive for God's kingdom, and food and clothing—everything you need—will be given to you.

It is a beautiful, hope-filled, life-giving passage . . . unless your rent is due on Tuesday and you don't have the money to pay it and you conclude that you, therefore, must not be doing what God requires of you.

It is a beautiful, hope-filled, life-giving passage . . . unless you have so many possessions that you've had to build a bigger barn to hold them all and you conclude that you, therefore, must be doing precisely what God requires of you.

We get things turned around so easily. That's what happens when those who are fortunate by the world's standards think, "I must be doing something right, and therefore God is on my side." And that's what happens when those who are less fortunate by the world's standards think, "I must be doing something wrong. God is not on my side." Both statements are testaments to greed.

In response, God says, "You fool."

God announced to rich and to poor that the numbers on W-2 forms don't matter. The message of the passage is that our trinkets and toys, our stuff and possessions are not fit subjects for worship, not fit subjects for the fullness of our attention. Only God is God, and only God is to be worshiped. If we believe that God treasures us, we may still have a savings account, but we won't pretend that our security rests in a bank. If we believe that God treasures us, we may still be behind on the rent, but we won't define ourselves by our difficulties.

Think of Isaiah 43:4, where God says, "You are precious in my sight, and honored, and I love you." Think of Hosea, where God was to Israel "like those who lift infants to their cheek. I bent down to them and fed them." Think of the ravens and the lilies, how God provides for them, and how much more God wants to provide for you.

God's love is not based on what we have or do not have, or what we do or do not do. God's love is based on who God is. We can't earn God's love; it's already present. We can't increase God's love; it's already full. And we can't deserve or warrant God's love, because God loves us undeservedly.

If we trust in God's love, we can leave behind our anxiety about money and possessions. If we trust in God's love, we can join the theological student in Hiroshima in saying, "It's funny, but things (left shoes, right shoes, money) don't matter anymore." We can claim that truth in the face of the promises of God—God who calls us by name, God who lifts us like infants to God's cheek, God who bends down and feeds us.

Amen.

SUGGESTIONS FOR WORSHIP

Call to Worship (Ps. 73:1-5, 23-26)

LEADER: Truly God is good to the upright,
to those who are pure in heart.

PEOPLE: **But as for me, my feet had almost stumbled;
my steps had nearly slipped.**

LEADER: For I was envious of the arrogant;
I saw the prosperity of the wicked.

PEOPLE: **For they have no pain;
their bodies are sound and sleek.**

LEADER: They are not in trouble as others are;
they are not plagued like other people.

PEOPLE: **Nevertheless I am continually with you;
you hold my right hand.**

LEADER: You guide me with your counsel,
and afterward you will receive me with honor.

PEOPLE: **Whom have I in heaven but you? And there is nothing on earth
that I desire other than you.**

LEADER: My flesh and my heart may fail,

PEOPLE: **But God is the strength of my heart and my portion forever.**

(*The New Testament and Psalms: An Inclusive Version* [New York: Oxford University Press, 1995])

Prayer of Confession

Mender God,
we bring to you
torn and ragged lives,
our communities fraying at the seams,
the cuffs and collars.
Won't you take your hand to us?
Won't you look us over,
see what can be done?
Mender, maker, seamstress God,
shake us out, straighten those crooked hems,
    mend the ragged, gaping tears.
Mender, maker, seamstress God,
Make this garment whole again. Amen.

(Johanna W. H. van Wijk-Bos, *Re-Imagining God: The Case for Scriptural Diversity* [Louisville: Westminster/John Knox Press, 1995], p. 48)

Benediction

God be in your head, and in your understanding.
God be in your eyes, and in your looking.
God be in your mouth, and in your speaking.
God be in your heart, and in your thinking.
God be in your end, and at your departing.

(Sarum Liturgy, *The United Methodist Book of Worship* [Nashville: The United Methodist Publishing House, 1992], 566)

Ordinary Time 21 or Proper 16

Mary Ellen Azada

Jeremiah 1:4-10: This passage tells of Jeremiah's call to be a prophet. Clearly we see God's grace reverberating throughout this passage. Nothing Jeremiah did brought him this call. Before Jeremiah is even born, God has appointed him "a prophet to the nations."

Psalm 71:1-6: The psalmist calls upon God for deliverance, rescue, and protection. He reminds God in this hour of distress that it was God who initiated this call and in obedience to that call, the psalmist has sought after God. Therefore, the psalmist reasons, pleads, and reminds God that the predicament he is in requires God's intervention. The psalmist calls upon God to act with justice, mercy, and kindness on his behalf.

Hebrews 12:18-29: Chapter 12 begins with the well-known metaphor of the Christian life as a race. In order to encourage the Hebrews, the writer focuses on the trials and temptations of life as a means for growth and discipline. But the passage takes an interesting twist in that it also warns believers not to reject God. The writer steps back and attempts to reframe our perspective on the Christian life. The God whom we are called to serve is the God of *all creation.* In widening the lens, the writer most certainly causes us to pause and refocus on God.

Luke 13:10-17: This is the third Sabbath controversy that appears in Luke's Gospel. The first incident occurs in the synagogue and revolves around the healing of the man who had an unclean demon (4:31-27). The second is the healing of the man with a withered hand

(6:6-11). And, in this passage, the story is told of the bent-over woman. These stories focus not only on God's healings (spiritual, physical, emotional, and psychosocial), but on the Jesus who gives this woman a new sense of self and renames her "daughter of Abraham."

REFLECTIONS

When we consider what it means to be called by God, several different images come to us from scripture. We recall the young boy Samuel lying in the Temple. When he hears a voice in the middle of the night, he assumes it is the old priest Eli. But instead he learns it is God (1 Samuel 3). Or Moses, busy watching his father-in-law's flock, finds God calling him from a burning bush. Or Mary, going about the tasks for women of that day and age, is greeted by an angel of God giving her the news that she will carry the very Son of the Most High (Luke 1).

Whatever the situation, God initiates and calls. Those called were no brighter than others—no better prepared to hear God's call. They were called by God's grace.

When I read these passages, I was struck by the theme of "call" that seems to rise from them. God calls the woman in Luke "daughter of Abraham." God calls Jeremiah "prophet to the nations." In Psalms and Hebrews, the notion of call is also placed in the context of God's domain.

Because God does the calling, we can be set free to know that the God who calls is also the God who will prepare and lead those called through all things.

A SERMON BRIEF

Jesus is in the synagogue teaching and, like preachers looking out over the modern congregation, his eyes scan the crowd. They stop when he sees a woman bent over and crippled. In her eyes, he discerns that she has had a spirit that has left her unable to stand up straight for eighteen years. I can imagine Jesus seeing the lines etched in her face and deciphering what emotion lay behind them. Most of all, I see Jesus looking upon her with compassion.

Unlike others who tried to reach Jesus for healing, whether by being lowered through a roof or by touching the hem of his cloak, this woman remains where she is and Jesus goes to her and says, "Woman, you are set free from your ailment." So saying, he lays his hands upon her.

I recall as a teenager growing up in Asia seeing women in their eighties and nineties walking down the street bent over, walking ever so slowly. I wondered if that was going to be my plight when I reached that age. I remember stretching my back whenever I felt myself hunched over and, of course, the frequent reminders from my mother to sit up straight kept that picture of those elderly women alive in my mind. Even though osteoporosis was not something known to them then, I was keenly aware of their condition and empathized with them. I remember one serious attempt I made in the hopes of preventing that condition. I found some twine and measured it and tied the two ends together. Then I threaded one arm into the circle of twine, and then the other arm so that it became a makeshift harness of sorts that went across the top of my shoulders and below my shoulder blades. I imagined in the same way that orthodontic gear was used to pull back my teeth, this twine would keep my shoulders from lurching forward. Fortunately, this "treatment" for my back did not last long as this was definitely not a comfortable way to be a teenager.

Imagine what kind of life these bent-over women must have had. To view the world from a bent position, one would have to continually turn one's head from side to side or move one's entire body to get a better view of things. Imagine the neck pain and the strain of sore muscles after eighteen years with such an ailment.

So Jesus heals this woman on the Sabbath. But this story is about more than the breaking—or not breaking—of the commandment against work on the Sabbath. This story moves us to an ever deeper understanding of who Jesus is as he makes a simple observation and leads us to a God who sees all of life, the contradictions, hypocrisies, and hardnesses of our hearts.

Jesus punctuates this healing with the observation that owners of a beast of burden would at least untie their animal and lead it to water, even on the Sabbath. Certainly, the donkey or ox would be important for their livelihood and transportation. Without animals, the humans' work would be greatly limited or at least hampered. There would be a heavy price to pay if the animal died. A farmer without an ox would only be able to manage a small portion of land, thereby limiting his income.

And Jesus must have seen many who did break the Sabbath to care for their animals. Jesus sees behind their words. Behind their veil of what appeared to be a religious desire to follow God and God's commands lay an insidious disregard for women, and persons who were ill.

For unlike work animals, the bent-over woman had absolutely no value in this society. With a flippant remark, the leader of the synagogue could easily condemn Jesus and what he did for her. His remark said more about how he felt about that woman, and perhaps all women of that day, than it did about Jesus' healing on the Sabbath. She was of less value than the ox or donkey.

Jesus hears and sees the condition of the hearts of his opponents. He addresses their callousness and their hate. Then he turns the law on its head and makes it clear how rigid the leaders of that day were. Their concern for the law went only so far as it benefited them economically.

But Jesus also sees this woman and the condition of her heart. He gives her back her dignity, her ability to be productive in society, her very soul! And then he frees her from this bondage and calls her a "daughter of Abraham."

The story doesn't say whatever became of this woman, but I can imagine a woman who is given a new life. Perhaps for the very first time she understands her value to God, not for what she could or could not do, but merely because she was a daughter of Abraham, a child of God!

Jesus saw clearly the condition of her heart as well as that of the leaders. He could read what was in each person. In the leaders' heart he saw pride, arrogance, and reliance upon self. In the woman's heart he saw perhaps frustration, helplessness, and loss of control. Jesus had mercy upon her.

For me, the question this story brings up is, have I allowed the law—or something else that I hold sacred—to stand in the way of compassion? How does one balance the two? Can we hold on to a "truth" without mistreating those needing to be loved?

The most powerful and life-giving action I believe Jesus took was not only to bring healing, but also to give the bent-over woman a new sense of who she was. After years of being beaten down with the belief that she was of no value, Jesus affirms her whole sense of being. What a gift and a miracle!

I cannot help thinking about my own sense of call as I read these passages. During the dinner celebrating my graduation from seminary, a relative asked me a rather serious question. "Why did you take back your maiden name?" He could not understand why I had chosen to take my name back in light of the fact that I was happily married! I answered, "I've always wanted to keep the name I was born with because I want to honor my parents. As immigrants to this country, my parents have sacrificed much to give me an education and a life. I want people to know that who I am and what I have become is because of my parents." With tears in his eyes, he nodded and said nothing more.

The power of a name, the power of a call from God, the power of the knowledge of being chosen by God, even before we are born, can and does transform us and gives us the courage to move forward, whatever the circumstances.

SUGGESTIONS FOR WORSHIP

Call to Worship (based on Ps. 71:1-6; Jer. 1:4-10)

LEADER: In you, O Lord, we take our refuge,

PEOPLE: **In you, O Lord, we find our strength.**

LEADER: We praise you, God, that before we were born, you knew us.

PEOPLE: **Upon you, we have leaned from our births.**

LEADER: Be for us our Rock and our Fortress.

PEOPLE: **And may our praise be continually for you.**

LEADER: Draw us near and touch our mouths

PEOPLE: **That we may speak of your greatness to all whom you send.**

ALL: **Praise the Lord!**

Prayer of Confession

All-knowing God,
Forgive us for we have sinned against you.
We confess that at times we are people with self-serving motives.
We speak as though we carry your truth for others,
while secretly we disobey your very intent for us.
Rid us of the desire to put ourselves before you and others.
Carve out of our very souls a place for honesty, integrity, and truth.
As we see ourselves, give us the power to live resurrected lives, full of grace, mercy, and love. May we yield our lives to the power of the Holy Spirit and to the fullness of Jesus Christ, our Lord and Savior. Amen.

Assurance of Pardon

Trust and believe in the Good News of Jesus Christ, the one who sees our repentant hearts, the one who forgives us when we call upon him.
Praise God, who calls us his own!

Benediction (based on Luke 13:16; Heb. 12:28)

Daughter of Abraham, son of Abraham, go forth into this world changed, for you are forgiven and are called children of God. We have received a kingdom that cannot be shaken. Therefore, let us live thankful lives filled with the reverence and awe due our Almighty God and Savior! Amen.

Ordinary Time 24 or Proper 19

Mary Cartledge-Hayes

Jeremiah 4:11-12, 22-28: The prophet warns of the coming of the "foe from the north." In the midst of descriptions of desolation, a note of hope sounds: "Yet I will not make a full end" (v. 27*b*).

Psalm 14: This psalm affirms that, in the face of pernicious evil, God is "with the company of the righteous."

I Timothy 1:12-17: The writer expresses gratitude for the mercy shown when he was a sinner and because he was a sinner. The mercy shown has allowed him to be an example for others.

Luke 15:1-10: Asked why he hangs around with sinners, Jesus tells the parables of a woman searching for one lost coin and a shepherd searching for one lost sheep, concluding each with a reference to the celebrations in heaven when a sinner repents.

REFLECTIONS

The Lukan lectionary reading shows the Pharisees and scribes grumbling over the time Jesus spends hanging out with sinners. Jesus responds with the parables of the lost coin and the lost sheep. These stories have dual emphases: celebration and repentance. A major exegetical question is whether to expand the sermon to include the third parable in the trilogy, that of the lost (prodigal) son. The first two parables point to the answer: each concludes with a reference to the celebration in heaven when sinners repent, a theme expanded and enfleshed in the parable of the lost son.

We are told twice in this reading, and a third time in the ensuing parable, that God celebrates when a sinner is found. How do we make clear what warrants such a celebration? Societal demands on women, and the finely drawn role boundaries that exist, often find us repenting over trivialities: a bag of potato chips eaten, a child's bath skipped, a report done well but not perfectly. This passage allows an opportunity to draw lines between what issues have salvific import and what are artificial constructs. An artist once told me of taking a charcoal class with a professor who seldom entered the room. Instead, he would open the door, yell in, "Go darker!" and proceed on his way. Just as charcoal drawings must "go darker" for the light to be visible, so must the preacher find a way to show the darkness so the light will be revealed. Naming the steps in repentance is one way of going darker.

A Sermon Brief

I have a friend who loves God a lot. She trusts God, listens to the leading of the Holy Spirit in her decisions, studies scripture, and celebrates all that God has done in her life and in the world. She's really very happy with God, except for one thing.

She's joking—but only half-joking—when she asks, "What good is a God who loves everyone? I want God to love me best of all."

I don't think she's alone in feeling that way. A lot of us want God to love us best of all. Of course, a lot of us just keep hoping that God loves us as much as God loves everyone else, that we're not going to be left out. We don't even dare to imagine that it might make God happy to count us in.

Religious leaders seem to be good at counting people in and out. In today's passage they were grumbling because trashy people—tax collectors and sinners—kept showing up to hear Jesus. They didn't like it. Jesus wanted the religious leaders to understand something about God they didn't know, so Jesus told them three stories.

A shepherd, he said, had a hundred sheep. One of them wandered away. The shepherd ignored his ninety-nine well-behaved sheep and went looking for the one that was lost. When he found it, he threw a party. He got in touch with all his friends and said, "Come on! It's time to celebrate! I've found my lost sheep!"

A woman had ten coins. She lost one. She ignored her nine coins, the ones safe in her pocket, and she went looking for the one that was lost. She got her broom, and she lit her lamp, and she searched all over the house. When she found the tenth coin, she threw a party. She got in touch with all her friends and said, "Come on! It's time to celebrate! I've found my coin!"

A third story goes along with the first two. In that story, a man had two sons, and he lost one. He didn't misplace his son, like the woman with the coin. The son just kind of wandered off, like the sheep. The son went away with his inheritance, cash money from his dad, in his pocket. He went to the city and blew all the money, and then the world turned against him: a famine came, and there was no food. Things got so bad the son hired himself out to feed pigs, which was about the most disgusting job a Jew could hold. The son was so hungry he'd have eaten the pigs' food if he could have.

And then one day the son changed. He repented. That means he did three things. First he looked at his life, at who he was and what he'd done, and he measured his life against the life to which he was called. The second thing he did was feel truly sorry at how thoroughly he'd fallen short. The third thing he did was make a decision to leave his old life behind and to start a new life, a life in which he would live into and up to a higher standard.

After he repented, the son went home. When he got there, his dad threw a party. His dad called all the neighbors and said, "Come on! It's time to celebrate! I've found my son!"

There's a little more to the story. It turns out the dad had another son, a perfect son, a good boy who did what was right his whole life. The perfect son got his feelings hurt when he saw this big party going on for his trashy brother.

Some people get really irritated with this story. Maybe it's because they try to be perfect and think God really should love them best of all as a result. Or maybe they just think it's not fair. Maybe they don't begrudge the party for the wandering son so much as wish that just once someone would throw a party for them.

The message of this passage, though, doesn't have to do with people who are perfect and need a little appreciation. The reality is that none of us is a perfect son. We're all made in the image of God, but we've all fallen short of the glory of God. We all sin. No matter how hard we try to be perfect, we just can't get it right. Time after time after time we fall short.

Listen again to what Jesus said: "There will be more joy in heaven over one sinner who repents than over ninety-nine righteous persons who need no repentance." And now ask yourself: Where are those ninety-nine people who need no repentance? Who are they, the ninety-nine who have no need to look at their lives and ask where they're falling short, who have no need to turn around, to enter anew into a commitment to living as God would have them live, to loving as God would have them love? Where are the ninety-nine perfect ones?

My friends, they don't exist. We are all human, and that means we all fall short; we all wander away from what God desires of us. We all sin, and we all need to repent.

So what is Jesus saying here, if he's not setting up a conflict between those who sin and those who don't, between wandering sons and stay-at-home sons? Listen again: "There is . . . joy in heaven over one sinner who repents" and later "there is joy in the presence of the angels of God over one sinner who repents." In other words, when one person repents, God calls all the neighbors and says, "Come on! It's time to celebrate!"

Since it makes God so happy, you'd think we'd just get on with it. We'd all repent once a day or so and sleep well at night, knowing we'd been the source of the angels dancing in heaven. The trouble is that repenting is so hard. Each one of the three steps is hard.

First of all, repentance is about really big things. It's not about changing our personalities or ignoring our emotions or never being in a bad mood or never being angry with someone for a good reason. Repentance is about the whopping big spiritual questions, the questions we forget as soon as we walk out the church door. Questions like: Have I fed the widows and orphans? Have I visited those in prison? Have I shown mercy? Have I loved my neighbor as myself? Have I loved myself? Have I loved the Lord my God with all my heart and all my soul and all my mind?

The second step is just as hard. We've got to feel sorry. We don't have to feel guilty or embarrassed; we just have to feel sorry. But it's not like an "I'm sorry I stepped on your foot" sorry. Repentance requires that we be truly sorry, that we feel deep-in-the-bone sorrow for what we've done or not done, that we feel real grief that we haven't lived the life God calls us to live.

The third step isn't any easier than the first two. The third step is making a decision to act differently, to live differently. It means committing our lives to caring for those widows and orphans, or committing our lives to showing mercy, or committing our lives to loving our neighbor as ourselves, or to loving God with all our heart and all our soul and all our mind. As we grow in grace, it may even mean doing all those things at the same time.

Repentance—real repentance—is just plain hard. But it isn't impossible, because of who God is. God is like the shepherd who lost one sheep. God is like the woman who lost one coin. God is searching for us, constantly searching, endlessly drawing us nearer. When we notice—and when we respond—God will say, "Come on! It's time to celebrate!"

SUGGESTIONS FOR WORSHIP

Call to Worship (based on Ps. 145:1*a*, 2, 5, 6*b*, 8, 10)

LEADER: I praise you my God.

PEOPLE: **I praise you every day.**

LEADER: I praise your name forever and ever.

PEOPLE: **Your majesty and glory are wonderful.**

LEADER: I will tell about your miracles.

PEOPLE: **I will tell about the great things you do.**

LEADER: The Lord is kind and merciful.

PEOPLE: **The Lord is patient and full of love.**

LEADER: Lord, the things you do bring praise to you.

PEOPLE: **Your followers bless you.**

(Excerpted from *The Holy Bible: English Version for the Deaf* [Grand Rapids, Mich.: Baker Book House, 1987, 1989, 1992])

Prayer of Confession

Almighty God, we confess that we are often swept up in the tide of our generation. We have failed in our calling to be your holy people, a people set apart for your divine purpose. We live more in apathy born of fatalism than in passion born of hope. We are moved more by private ambition than by social justice. We dream more of privilege and benefits than of service and sacrifice. We try to speak in your name without relinquishing our glories, without nourishing our souls, without relying wholly on your grace. Help us to make room in our hearts and lives for you. Forgive us, revive us, and reshape us in your image. Amen.

(From *1987 United Methodist Clergywomen's Consultation Resource Book,* p. 57, written by Rev. Lydia S. Martinez)

Benediction

May the presence of God the Creator give you strength;
May the presence of God the Redeemer give you peace;
May the presence of God the Sustainer give you comfort.
May the presence of God the Sanctifier give you love. Amen.

(From *1987 United Methodist Clergywomen's Consultation Resource Book,* p. 67)

Ordinary Time 27 or Proper 22

Ann L. Petker

Lamentations 1:1-6: This passage represents a portion of a collection of five laments which describe, in great detail, the conditions of life following the destruction of Jerusalem.

Psalm 137: This psalm is a text of pain and remembrance about the exile in Babylon.

II Timothy 1:1-14: The writer lifts up the life of faith. It is a life marked by a spirit of power, love, and self-discipline. "Guard the good treasure entrusted to you, with the help of the Holy Spirit."

Luke 17:5-10: This pericope is composed of two sections. The first, verses 5-6, is the well-known saying in which faith is compared to a mustard seed. The second, verses 7-10, is a complex text involving a slave owner and a slave. This section challenges us to consider our role vis-à-vis God.

REFLECTIONS

One of the issues that arises for most of us who seek to lead faithful lives is the fear that comes from openly sharing our faith. No matter how strong our convictions are, many of us are truly afraid to tell others about the Good News contained within the gospel. We struggle because we know that God calls us to witness about Jesus Christ, yet we fear the consequences if we do.

I know I have found comfort and inspiration numerous times in this passage from II Timothy. I need to be reminded constantly to "rekindle the gift of God that is within me." It is important for us as pastors to share with our congregations our own struggles and fears, thus enabling us to "journey together" through the difficulties of a life of faith. We are all of us "in this together." We are learning together how to spread the good news of God's love, and we are not alone on our journey. God has called us on this journey and gives us a "spirit of power and of love and of self-discipline." What incredible news to share with our congregations. We have been entrusted with the "good treasure" and charged to guard it well with the "help of the Holy Spirit living in us."

A SERMON BRIEF

Every night when I was a child, my father and I had a ritual we went through before I went to sleep. Silly as it sounds, I found it to be very reassuring. Before he turned out the light, he would go over to the closet door, open it up, peek inside, and say, "Anybody in there?" (He was asking for any monsters who might have stopped by to acknowledge their presence.) Hearing no replies, he would close the closet door and wish me good night. What can I say? It worked. What worked about this ritual, as I analyze it as an adult, was the fact that my father didn't ridicule my fears. He didn't say, "Snap out of it. You know there are no monsters in your closet." Instead he acknowledged, by his actions, that he knew my fears were very real, and he loved me through them. Many years later I gave him a poster—which now hangs in his office—that has pink, goofy monsters on it. The caption underneath reads, "From ghoulies and ghosties and things that go bump in the night . . . Lord, deliver us."

O Lord, deliver us from our fear. Fear. One of my favorite quotes from one of my favorite books, A. A. Milne's *Winnie the Pooh*, describes how I often feel. "Piglet," said Rabbit, taking out a pencil and licking the end of it, "you haven't any pluck." "It is hard to be brave," said Piglet, sniffing slightly, "when you're only a very small animal" (*Winnie the Pooh*, E. P. Dutton & Co., Inc., 1926, copyright renewal, 1954). Sometimes it is very hard to be brave.

It's hard to be brave in a world where the scandals of televangelists and local pastors have tainted people's view of the church. It's hard to be brave in our very secular world where the church has been usurped by people's busy schedules, New Age religions, and a general cynicism toward organized religion. It's hard to speak up for the church, it's hard to share our faith, sometimes it's even hard to admit we are Christians, in a secular setting. Rabbit might as well be saying to us, "Church, you haven't any pluck."

It's not that we don't want to be brave, but it is just very hard. I recently took a class on becoming an advocate for victims of domestic violence, and let me tell you, the church did not fare well there. Far too many of the attendees had had their own experiences or heard of instances where pastors had told the victims to remember their marriage vows, to stay with their abusers, and pray. I found myself wishing numerous times that I had not identified myself as a pastor, and I found myself needing extra courage to speak up and say, "Not all churches, not all pastors will respond that way." It's hard to be brave in the face of anger against the church.

In this letter to Timothy, the acknowledgment of the fear of speaking out is addressed. Timothy is reminded of the sincere faith of his grandmother, Lois, and of his mother, Eunice—the faith that is now his—the faith that has been handed down through the generations. The faith of his family was handed down to him through their actions, through their words, and they assured him of the Lord's deliverance of us.

Thus reminded of the strength of his faith, Timothy is encouraged to "rekindle the gift of God that is within [him]." He is reminded of the gift of the Holy Spirit that was given him—the gift of the Holy Spirit who lives in each of us. Rekindle this Spirit—it filled your grandmother and your mother—this Spirit has filled the saints through the ages. And what an incredible gift. "For God did not give us a spirit of cowardice, but rather a spirit of power and of love and of self-discipline." It's hard to be brave, but all whom God has called possess "a Spirit of power and love."

In his book *Stride Toward Freedom,* the Reverend Martin Luther King, Jr., describes a religious experience he had. He describes the various threats that had been made on his life and family. "In this state of exhaustion, when my courage had all but gone, I decided to take my problem to God," he wrote. He sat at the kitchen table in his home and prayed, confessing that he did not know if he could provide the kind of courageous leadership needed. Fear had sapped his energy. In that act of surrender, something happened. He wrote, "At that moment I experienced the presence of the Divine as I had never experienced him before. It seems as though I could hear the quiet assurance of an inner voice saying, 'Stand up for righteousness, stand up for truth; and God will be at your side forever.' Almost at once my fears began to go. My uncertainty disappeared. I was ready to face anything." A few days later while he was out of town, his home was bombed. "Strangely enough," he said, "I accepted the word of the bombing calmly. My religious experience a few nights before had given me the strength to face it" (*Stride Toward Freedom,* New York: Harper and Brothers, 1958, pp. 134-36). It is not hard to be brave when the Spirit of God is on fire within us.

We know that living the Christian life in the midst of this society is not easy. The Christian life has never been easy. At times, we, as millions of

Christians before us, may suffer and struggle because of our faith. But we have been given "the good treasure." We know the saving love of God through Jesus. We know the power of the gospel. "Don't be ashamed, then," writes Paul in his letter to Timothy, "of the testimony about our Lord, but join with me in suffering for the gospel, relying on the power of God, who saved us and called us with a holy calling."

I know it is hard to be brave when you feel like a very small person in the middle of this big world—but "guard the good treasure entrusted to you, with the help of the Holy Spirit living in us."

You and the world will be blessed. Amen.

SUGGESTIONS FOR WORSHIP

Call to Worship

LEADER: People of God, rejoice! For we have been given a spirit of power.

PEOPLE: We will rejoice in God!

LEADER: People of God, give thanks! For we have been given a spirit of love.

PEOPLE: We will give thanks to God!

LEADER: People of God, celebrate! For we have been given a spirit of self-discipline.

PEOPLE: We will celebrate God's gifts to us!

LEADER: Let us worship God, who through Jesus Christ has saved us and called us with a holy calling according to God's purposes.

ALL: Let us worship God!

Prayer of Confession

God of grace, we confess that we turn our hearts from you and focus upon ourselves—we live in fear of what others may think of us, of what the consequences for us may be if we share our faith in you. We fail to share the good treasure you have entrusted to us because we rely on our own abilities instead of your power. Forgive us and empower us again to claim your courage and your love that we may be your faithful disciples in the world. Through Jesus Christ we pray. Amen.

Assurance of Pardon

Children of God, receive the good news of the gospel: in Jesus Christ we are forgiven and made new. We do not need to be afraid—God is with us. Thanks be to God!

Benediction

May you be filled with God's spirit of power and love, and the knowledge that God is with you always. You need not be afraid. Amen.

Ordinary Time 28 or Proper 23

Catherine Gunsalus González

Jeremiah 29:1, 4-7: The exiles in Babylon are told to build houses, plant gardens, and seek the welfare of the city in which they are living.

Psalm 66:1-12: God is praised for deliverance in the past through the sea and for a new deliverance in answer to the psalmist's prayers.

2 Timothy 2:8-15: The word of God is not chained. We can be sure that if we have died with Christ Jesus, we will live with him; if we endure, we will reign with him; if we deny him, he will deny us; if we are faithless, he remains faithful. Thus, we may be workers who are not ashamed.

Luke 17:11-19: The cleansing of the ten lepers.

REFLECTIONS

Jesus and his disciples were traveling on the border between Galilee and Samaria. They were Galileans and were therefore considered authentically Jewish, although many Jews in Jerusalem considered Galileans definitely second-class Jews in comparison to those in the capital city, who were closer to the Temple and the priesthood. But Samaritans were a different matter. Jews in general, including those in Galilee, did not consider them really Jewish at all. There had been too much intermarriage with the other populations there, and the Samaritans did not worship in Jerusalem, but rather at the ancient shrine in Shechem. In the Gospel of John the woman at the well says to Jesus: " 'How is it that you, a Jew, ask a drink of me, a woman of Samaria?' For Jews have no dealings with Samaritans" (John 4:9*b* RSV); and, "Our ancestors worshiped on this mountain; but you say that the place where people must worship is in Jerusalem" (John 4:20). Obviously, there was great distrust between the two groups, and there were religious differences of significant proportions. We catch some of that difference earlier in the Gospel of Luke, in the parable of the good Samaritan, where it is astonishing that a Samaritan, one of that despised people, is actually the one who acts as the neighbor to the man who fell among thieves on the road from Jerusalem to Jericho, a city just over the border into Samaria. It is not insignificant that the story of the ten lepers is set on the border between Galilee and Samaria.

What the account does not tell us at first is that the group of lepers is a mixed group. There are Jews and at least one Samaritan. Evidently, their status as lepers overcomes any hesitation they have at associating with each other. Since lepers are outcasts in the Jewish community, and probably in the Samaritan community as well, they might just as well form a single community of outcasts! As long as they are all lepers, what does it matter?

A Sermon Brief

On the surface, this story seems simple and straightforward, pointing to the virtue of gratitude. It's almost as though scripture were a parent speaking to children, urging them to say "thank you" when someone has done something nice for them. Even Jesus appreciates a "thank you."

But a few minutes really studying these few verses make it clear that its meaning is far more complex than a simple "always say 'thank you,' even to God."

What seems to matter to Jesus is not so much the thanking as the glorifying of God. The text says that the Samaritan was doing that with a loud voice, even before he thanked Jesus. And Jesus' concern about the other nine is not that they did not thank him, but that they did not give glory to God. Couldn't they have given glory to God without coming back to Jesus? Evidently not. What is at issue here is not a spirit of gratitude to someone who does something helpful—even lifesaving—for them. What matters is the recognition that it is God who has acted and that the way God has acted so dramatically is in the ministry of Jesus. The issue is the recognition of who this Jesus is. The nine who keep on going are probably quite grateful that they have been healed, but their healing has evidently taught them nothing about who Jesus is. The Samaritan recognized that somehow, in this Galilean preacher and healer, God is acting in a new and unique way. The priests can wait—and with that, also his acceptance back into society. What matters most is the astonishing presence of God in the one who had sent him to the priests. He feels compelled to go back because of this realization.

And Jesus wonders out loud why it is that it is the Samaritan, the foreigner, who has understood. That is a good question for us to ponder as well. Were the Jews so familiar with the ways of God, so knowledgeable about what was to be done, that they failed to recognize this new action? If so, we stand in the same danger, for we too are those who know and study the ways of God. Perhaps there is a religious familiarity that makes it difficult really to be astonished. Perhaps that is why so often Jesus indicates that harlots and tax collectors would enter the kingdom before the religious people of the day. The people who assumed they were outcasts from the God of Israel—the harlots, the tax collectors, the lepers, the Samaritans—were more ready to be astonished by God's love and mercy.

But perhaps the most surprising and clarifying statement in this passage is the very last verse. After Jesus comments on the absence of the nine, he then speaks to the Samaritan: "Rise and go your way; your faith has made you [whole]" (Luke 17:19*b* RSV).

The man was already healed. What does it mean that his faith has made him whole? The words here are quite different. About the leprosy, the words used are "cleansed" or "healed." But the Samaritan's faith has made him whole; these words can also be translated, "his faith has saved him." Ten were healed. For ten, the leprosy was cured. But for one—the one who returned, the one who realized, however vaguely, who Jesus was—his faith in this one in whom he glimpsed God—his faith, not his gratitude—saved him.

This passage immediately precedes descriptions of the kingdom of God. There will be a suddenness about the coming of the kingdom. It will be like the time of Noah, when, for Noah's neighbors, life went on as usual, while for Noah the last days were present. People will ask about when to expect the kingdom, only to be told it is in their midst. Noah recognized the kingdom and changed his life because of it. The Samaritan leper recognized the dawning kingdom in Jesus, and everything else was secondary, even his own leprosy. His faith, obvious in his actions, made him whole. The other nine ceased to be lepers. Most likely, they continued on their way to Jerusalem. They were examined by the priests and certified as healthy. They could now be full members of society. Life could go on. Surely they were grateful to God and grateful to Jesus. They had their old lives back. But they had missed the kingdom of God that had been in their midst in the person of Jesus. Their lives were healed, but old. The Samaritan had also been healed. But what he had was a new life, not a new lease on an old life.

This passage is not about gratitude. It is not about saying, "Thank you." It is about the nearness of the kingdom and the readiness to enter it. It is about being so caught up in our old lives that we fail to recognize the possibility of a new one. It is about the work of God in Jesus, who is not simply fixing up old lives, but offering new ones. It is about a wholeness, a salvation, that is far beyond healing—a wholeness, a salvation for the whole creation gone awry. And it is about the advantages that outsiders sometimes have in recognizing the presence of the kingdom.

Sometimes our hopes for healing are so limited that we miss all that God is offering to us in Christ. Perhaps those on the margins of society, those who are outcast, because their whole lives cry out for healing and wholeness—perhaps they are more open to the fullness of God's salvation.

SUGGESTIONS FOR WORSHIP

Call to Worship (Ps. 66:1-3*a*, 4 adapted)

LEADER: Make a joyful noise to God, all the earth;

PEOPLE: Sing the glory of God's name;

LEADER: Give to God glorious praise.

PEOPLE: Say to God: "How awesome are your deeds!

LEADER: All the earth worships you;

PEOPLE: They sing praises to you; they sing praises to your name."

Prayer of Confession

We confess, O God, that our prayers are so small when measured by all that you desire for us. Again and again we close our lives to your will when it does not fit our hopes. We forget you can be trusted to work for our good. Keep our faith lively, so that in the midst of all the confusion of our lives, we may not miss the presence of your kingdom. Astonish us with the newness of life that jolts us out of the ruts into which we settle so comfortably. All this we ask in the name of Jesus, who came that we might have life more abundantly than we could even imagine. Amen.

Sending Forth (Luke 17:19)

Hear and believe the words of Jesus: "Rise and go your way; your faith has made you [whole]" (RSV).

Thanksgiving Sunday

Margaret Moers Wenig

Deuteronomy 26:1-11: The Israelites receive instructions to bring to God the firstfruits of the land and to remember both their oppression in Egypt and God's deliverance.

Psalm 100: We are invited to "make a joyful noise to the Lord" and to remember that God made us and we belong to God.

Philippians 4:4-9: The "beloved" are encouraged to "rejoice in the Lord always," to let God know their requests, and to "think about" what is true, honorable, just, pure, pleasing, and commendable. And the peace of God will guard their hearts and minds.

John 6:25-35: Jesus' conversation with the crowd ends with his words, "I am the bread of life."

REFLECTIONS

The bringing of firstfruits in Deuteronomy 26:1-4 sounds like the Pilgrims' first harvest, which became our Thanksgiving, as well as, in an entirely different vein, the payment of income taxes. "I have come to this country, I have worked here, I have made some money, and now I pay a percentage of those earnings to the government as I am required."

Whether the offering of firstfruits is a voluntary thanksgiving offering or a form of tithe or tax, it is not surprising to find it here. What follows, however, is somewhat surprising. Why, when the taxes are paid or when the thanksgiving offering is presented, must the Israelite recite the following formula?

> My father was a fugitive Aramean. He went down to Egypt with meager numbers and sojourned there, but there he became a great and very populous nation. The Egyptians dealt harshly with us and oppressed us; they imposed heavy labor on us. We cried to the Lord, the God of our ancestors, and the Lord heard our plea and saw our plight, our misery, and our oppression. The Lord freed us from Egypt by a mighty hand, by an outstretched arm and awesome power, and by signs and portents. God brought us to this place and gave us this land, a land flowing with milk and honey. Wherefore I now bring the first fruits of the soil which You, O Lord, have given me. (Deuteronomy 26:5-10*a* TANAKH)

Wouldn't it have been sufficient simply to declare the income and pay the tax, or to reap the harvest and offer thanks?

A SERMON BRIEF

Why did Moses instruct the Israelites to recite a story about their past wanderings at the very moment they would be offering up the fruits of their present homeland? Perhaps it's because he knew that they wouldn't be able to forget their past, nor should they.

As recent immigrants to the land of Canaan, grateful to be settled in the land of milk and honey, wouldn't the Israelites be eager to forget their harsh past? Some might. Others might not. Their experience, the experience of their parents and grandparents in the land of Egypt, the hardships they suffered, the language they spoke, the music they played, and the food they ate, as well as their experience of migration, would long remain a part of them. That experience would remain a part of the identity of the immigrant generation and maybe even a part of the identity of subsequent generations.

What might your declaration sound like or the declarations of your neighbors?

My mother was a German Jew. Her ancestors went to the Rhineland few in numbers and sojourned there. But there they became a great and very prosperous nation. The Nazis dealt harshly with us and oppressed us. Miraculously, we escaped in 1933 and came to this land of safety.

Or: My father was a Russian Jew. The Russian army drafted Jewish boys who were barely teenagers. Miraculously, my father escaped the czar's army, left Russia, and arrived in this land of freedom in 1900.

Or: My father was a West Indian. My ancestors prospered there but the economy contracted and jobs became scarce. Miraculously, my father made his way here in 1970 to this land of opportunity.

Or: My mother was from Guatemala. But the dictatorship oppressed my people. Miraculously, my mother made her way here in 1980 to this land of democracy.

Or: My father was from Vietnam, but the war destroyed his town and killed most of his family. Miraculously, he made his way here in 1975 to this land of peace.

In the first half of the twentieth century we spoke of America as a "melting pot." We assumed that people could and would become entirely American. Differences would melt away. Distinct histories and cultural heritages, when stewed together, would blend and ultimately disappear.

Moses knew better. He knew that even once settled in the Promised Land, the Israelites would not be able to forget their past in Egypt. Instead of adjuring them to start afresh, to wipe the slate clean and assume a new identity, Moses commanded the people to remember their past.

Our past, our family's past, our people's past are part of who we are today. The immigrants to America of this generation know what a previous generation tried to deny. They struggle to preserve their culture, their music, their rituals, their diets, their language, as Moses would have the Israelites preserve their distinctive identity, too.

This promised land is not a melting pot—a single stew in which differences melt away. Rather America is more like an international buffet in which each immigrant group preserves its own distinctive history and culture.

No longer in the public schools is every child expected to say, falsely, "My father was a Pilgrim." Instead an immigrant child, or the child of immigrants has the freedom to say, without shame: "My father was a fugitive Aramean."

SUGGESTIONS FOR WORSHIP

Call to Worship (Psalm 100 adapted)

LEADER: Make a joyful noise to the Lord, all the earth.

PEOPLE: Worship the Lord with gladness;

LEADER: Come into God's presence with singing.

PEOPLE: Lord, we know that you are God.

LEADER: It is you who made us, and we belong to you.

PEOPLE: We are your people, the sheep of your pasture.

LEADER: We enter your gates with thanksgiving

PEOPLE: And your courts with praise.

LEADER: We give you thanks; we bless your name.

**ALL: For you, our Lord, are good;
            your steadfast love endures forever,
            and your faithfulness to all generations.**

Prayer of Confession

O God, forgive our forgetting. We forget that you made us and that we belong to you. We forget that our fathers and mothers were slaves in Egypt and that you delivered them and gave them a land flowing with milk and honey. We forget our own cries of fear or pain or despair and your deliverances. We forget to bring the firstfruits of all our work to you. We forget to rejoice. We forget to bring all our requests before you. We forget your promise of peace in our hearts and minds. And because we forget, our lives are frantic and fractured. Awaken us; turn us back to you—that in our remembering, our praying, our working, our giving, we may know your peace, promised to the whole world. Amen.

Benediction

The Lord bless you and keep you in your going out and your coming in.

Contributors

Charlotte McGruder Abram, Pastor, Union Memorial United Methodist Church, Omaha, Nebraska. Her partners in ministry include her husband, their three children, her mom, and the congregation. Even her two-year-old grandchild offers her support by shouting, "Amen!" when Grandma prays.

Mary Ellen Azada, Associate Pastor, First Presbyterian Church, Burlingame, California. "I am able to do what God has called me to do with the support and love of my husband, Gerald Chinen, who is a Presbyterian minister of another congregation. I am very lucky to have two church families that encourage me along this journey!"

Barbara Shires Blaisdell, Senior Minister, Central Christian Church (Disciples of Christ), Indianapolis, Indiana. Barbara is the first clergywoman to be called as senior minister of this historic 163-year-old congregation located in downtown Indianapolis. An avid gardener and mother of four, Barbara is currently busy collaborating on a book entitled *Theology for Preaching: Authority, Truth, and Knowledge of God in a Postmodern Ethos,* forthcoming from Abingdon Press.

Teresa L. Fry Brown, Associate Professor of Homiletics, Candler School of Theology, Emory University, Atlanta, Georgia. An ordained itinerate elder in the African Methodist Episcopal Church, Teresa is the first woman of color on Candler's faculty. Her husband, Frank, and her daughter, Veronica—the "wind beneath her wings"—help keep both her sanity and their house in order.

Mary Cartledge-Hayes, Pastor, Gravely Memorial United Methodist Church, Spartanburg, South Carolina. Mary is also a poet and the author of *To*

Love Delilah: Claiming the Women of the Bible. A former national coordinator of the Evangelical and Ecumenical Women's Caucus, she is active in domestic violence issues.

Catherine Gunsalus González, Professor of Church History, Columbia Theological Seminary, Decatur, Georgia. Catherine was ordained in the United Presbyterian Church (USA) in 1965. She and her husband, Justo González, live near campus in a house that is constantly being remodeled.

Susan Karen Hedahl, Associate Professor of Homiletics, Gettysburg Lutheran Theological Seminary, Gettysburg, Pennsylvania. Before moving to Gettysburg to teach, Sue was completing her doctoral work at the Graduate Theological Union in Berkeley, California. She observes that the move east was, in this case, not only a shift in geography, but in culture as well. Fortunately, she says, she "loves living in the city's nineteenth-century history"! She is a popular contributor to *Word and Witness* and numerous other preaching journals.

Lucy Lind Hogan, Assistant Professor of Preaching and Worship, Wesley Theological Seminary, Washington, D.C. Lucy is energized by the fact that she, a priest in the Episcopal Church, teaches at a United Methodist seminary that welcomes a truly ecumenical student body, everyone from Roman Catholics to Unitarian Universalists. Lucy lives in Maryland with her husband and her younger son; her older son is away at college.

Gail McDougle, Minister of Worship and Education, College Community Congregational Church (UCC), Fresno, California. Pastor, as well as mother and activist, Gail thrives on her busy life in a community where, after ten years of service, she is deeply committed to ecumenical and educational endeavors. Teen sons, Cullen and Jason, are her delights and reality anchors.

Agnes W. Norfleet, Pastor, North Decatur Presbyterian Church, Decatur, Georgia. When not doing church work, Agnes is with her two young sons at the zoo or on the site of a Habitat for Humanity house. Habitat plays an important role in the life of Agnes's family; her husband is the Executive Director of Habitat's Atlanta affiliate.

Ann L. Petker, Pastor, First Presbyterian Church, Myrtle Point, Oregon. Ann is a firm believer in the art of playing—an art she enjoys with her husband, two teen-age children, their friends, and a menagerie of pets. Collie-flower, her Border collie, serves as Ann's assistant in all areas of ministry.

Carter Shelley, Ph.D. candidate, Princeton Theological Seminary, Princeton, New Jersey. An ordained minister in the Presbyterian Church, Carter is currently combining a full-time vocation in childcare and the domestic arts with the writing of a doctoral dissertation. On any given weekday between the hours of 8:30 A.M. and 2:30 P.M., she can be found at the Wilkes County Public Library in Wilkesboro, North Carolina. Her vices include doughnuts, *Masterpiece Theater,* literary biographies, and the liberal use of large felt-tip pens in education and worship settings.

Christine M. Smith, Professor of Preaching and Worship, United Theological Seminary of the Twin Cities. She is author of *Weaving the Sermon: Preaching in a Feminist Perspective,* and *Preaching as Weeping, Confession and Resistance: Radical Responses to Radical Evil.*

Patricia A. Spearman, Senior Pastor, Jackson Chapel United Methodist Church, San Marcos, Texas. Patricia is an advocate of the social gospel with a strong record of community service. Although she is the official preacher in her family, she credits her sister, Donna, as the true theologian and is grateful for all the support she has received from her family and from a network of friends that spans the country.

Margaret Moers Wenig, Rabbi, Beth Am, The People's Temple, New York, New York; Instructor in Liturgy and Homiletics, Hebrew Union College— Jewish Institute of Religion. Maggie is the only Jewish member of the Academy of Homiletics, the professional association for those who teach preaching. She lives in New York with her partner and their two daughters.

Scripture Index

{ *Scripture Index* }

Subject Index